Assigning Blame

Assigning Blame

The Rhetoric of Education Reform

Mark Hlavacik

HARVARD EDUCATION PRESS
CAMBRIDGE, MASSACHUSETTS

Paperback ISBN 978-1-61250-972-3
Library Edition ISBN 978-1-61250-973-0

Library of Congress Cataloging-in-Publication Data

Names: Hlavacik, Mark, author.
Title: Assigning blame : the rhetoric of education reform / Mark Hlavacik.
Description: Cambridge, Massachusetts : Harvard Education Press, [2016] | Includes bibliographical references and index.
Identifiers: LCCN 2016018850| ISBN 9781612509723 (pbk.) | ISBN 9781612509730 (library edition)
Subjects: LCSH: Education and state—United States. | Educational change—United States. | Educational evaluation—United States.
Classification: LCC LC89 .H56 2016 | DDC 379.73—dc23
LC record available at https://lccn.loc.gov/2016018850

Published by Harvard Education Press,
an imprint of the Harvard Education Publishing Group

Harvard Education Press
8 Story Street
Cambridge, MA 02138

Cover Design: Wilcox Design
Cover Photo: iStock.com/adventtr

The typeface used in this book is Minion Pro.

To Brendon—

may words never fail you.

Contents

INTRODUCTION

Publicly Blaming: The Rhetoric of Education Reform

On October 17, 1979, President Jimmy Carter called members of both houses of Congress to the White House for the ceremonial signing of new legislation organizing a United States Department of Education (ED).[1] Along with several reporters and a class of fourth graders, the congressional delegation gathered in the East Room to bear witness as the president made history. For over a century, education had been a bureaucratic rolling stone. Although the small federal bureaucracy devoted to schooling was originally formed as a department by President Andrew Johnson in 1867, it was demoted to the status of office just two years later. As such, the US Office of Education bounced around the executive branch with no direct representative in the president's cabinet. For more than a century, as public schools proliferated across the country, their governance remained almost entirely the responsibility of state and local governments. Finally, in 1953, the Office of Education landed in the Department of Health, Education, and Welfare, wherefrom the assembled were to witness Carter liberate it.

Before putting pen to paper, the president addressed his East Room audience, explaining his reasons for restoring education to the status of department. According to Carter, public education in the United States suffered from a lack of coherent federal leadership. "The Federal Government," he lectured, has "confused its role of junior partner in American education with that of silent partner."[2] Comparing his experience lobbying for education reform as a Georgia state senator with his experience as president, Carter lamented: "When I became President, that situation was dramatically different. There has not been in the Federal Government an adequate mechanism by which we can improve the quality of education in the United States."[3] Having made his point, Carter turned his attention to corralling the unruly fourth graders and legislators for a photograph. Then, with everyone on their marks, he signed the bill.

With the department founded, Carter began speaking formally on behalf of the nation's newest and smallest cabinet-level agency. According to Carter, the most essential function of the ED would be to foster and direct the national deliberation over the purpose and shape of public schooling. "I came to the office of the Presidency determined," Carter said, "that our Nation's formidable educational challenges should be brought to the forefront of national discussion, where they belong."[4] Parsing the administrative purview of the new department from the role of the existing state-level departments, Carter explained that, unlike the state departments of education or the preceding federal office, the ED would create a "cabinet-level leader in education" to "stir national discussion of critical education concerns" and "increase the Nation's attention to education." Moreover, "as a result of placing education in a highly visible department of its own," Carter argued that the American people would gain "a much clearer perspective on what the Federal Government is doing in education." Carter characterized this more detailed perspective as a way to improve education policy making through democratization: "It allows people to better decide what the Government should and should not be doing in education."[5]

More than thirty years on, it is safe to say that Carter got his wish. There has been a vibrant and consequential deliberation over education policy centered on the role of the federal government in improving America's schools.[6] Not only has this conversation drawn participation from a multitude of perspectives and interests, it has resulted in dramatic policy changes. Whether they call it an "era," a "syndrome," or a "paradigm," scholars of education policy and history recognize the rise of accountability-based reforms as public education's defining development since the founding of the ED.[7] As they have worked to connect the dots between the publication of *A Nation at Risk* and the passage of No Child Left Behind, these scholars have written detailed accounts of the political transformation that precipitated a new kind of education policy during the closing decades of the twentieth century. But despite an abundance of scholarship analyzing the rise of accountability as a historical development or policy program, there is no sustained account of the persuasive tactics that facilitated such dramatic change.

This book looks closely at the visions that have competed for control of America's public school system since the founding of the ED in an effort to assess the national deliberation Carter solicited in the twilight of his presidency. Since 1980, public education in the United States has enjoyed a great deal of national attention, but on close examination much of that attention proves negative. For better and for worse, the failures of the public school system have been the fulcrum of the national deliberation Carter inaugurated along with the ED. Many Americans describe their public school system as failing, and so do the people they look to for leadership.[8] Regardless of its politics, nearly every organized effort to change education policy from the 1980s forward has agreed on the poor state of the public school system, each offering its own explanation for why. Voucher advocates have argued that public schools fail because they are monopolies. Social justice advocates have argued that public schools fail because they are segregated or otherwise unequal. The standards movement has argued that public schools fail because they have low expectations. The list goes on, but the rhetorical formula remains the same. Arguments for reform in the era of achievement begin by addressing the nagging question: Who or what is to blame for the unacceptable state of America's public schools?[9]

The consensus that America's schools are failing has made the public schools a rhetorical hot potato. By blaming, reformers put the burning roots of educational failure in someone else's hands. Blame gives reformers a tool that identifies a cause for educational failure to fit their preferred solution while simultaneously impugning rival interests. In this discursive landscape, blame is the high ground and the result has been the proliferation of blaming. Public education's blameworthy have included teachers, students, parents, administrators, and entire governments. Not even inanimate concepts like segregation, genetics, race, class, and progressivism have escaped the allegation of culpability. This profusion of blaming presents an opportunity to catalogue and compare blame's forms and their consequences as well as an opportunity to understand the patterns of public argument that have driven the contemporary politics of education. First, however, a word on the scholarly study of the history and politics of education.

A RHETORICAL HISTORY OF EDUCATION REFORM

In 1959, still twenty years before Carter founded his new department and foretold its deliberative future, a group of prominent historians gathered in Williamsburg, Virginia, for a meeting of the Institute of Early American History and Culture. Addressing "needs and opportunities for study," they discussed new approaches to the history of American education. Bernard Bailyn, a Harvard history professor, gave the keynote in which he argued for historical work that would appropriately situate North American educational practices in the context of their European forbears. Bailyn expressed special concern that the role of education in America's broader social history had been overlooked, to the detriment of both social and educational history. "Education," he observed, "not only reflects and adjusts to society; once formed, it turns back upon it and acts upon it. The consequences of this central transformation of education have significantly shaped the development of American society."[10] Although Bailyn made his remarks to encourage the study of educational practices in colonial America and during the early republic, his description of the give-and-take between American society and American education is at the heart of this project and a great deal of contemporary work on the history, policy, and sociology of education in the United States.

Now, after more than a century of near constant reform, academics who study education policy and history in the United States have begun an ambitious effort to approach their subject anew. Since the turn of the millennium, they have increasingly addressed the need for new perspectives on the meaning of public education in the United States. In particular, scholars have tried with mounting urgency to make sense of education policy's seemingly infinite appetite for reforms. In their efforts to do this, some scholars have declared reform the natural and rightful state of public education, whereas others have argued that reform is the chief influence ruining it. Some scholars have surveyed the history of reform and concluded that it is a broken record predictably revolving the same inadequate solutions, and still others have found distinct eras of reform forever layering policies and bureaucracies atop each other.[11] Implicitly, all of these scholars acknowledge reform as the unnamed mechanism in Bailyn's keynote, the social process through which American society acts upon education and education turns back upon it.

Through the politics of school reform, the United States and the public schools negotiate and renegotiate their indivisible future. Like all domains of public policy, education policy is created and enforced through the meaning-making power of language and argument.[12] When advocates and policy makers seek reforms, they turn to rhetoric to shape the public's perceptions and make a persuasive case for change. Rhetoric, which Aristotle defined as the "ability, in each [particular] case, to see the available means of persuasion," provides an intellectual tradition as well as a body of theory for analyzing the ethics and tactics of advocacy.[13] Indeed, many scholars have used rhetoric to analyze the public discussion of education policy and history.[14]

Applying the theoretical tools from rhetoric's scholarly tradition to the question of how best to understand an educational system stuck in perpetual reform, this book addresses the role of blame as the predominant persuasive resource of educational policy advocates. Blame anchors appeals for change, facilitating "reforming again, again, and again," by providing a narrative through which the expectations and outcomes of public education can be contested.[15] Far from a taboo or deviant persuasive technique, blame constitutes the core of education policy discourse. It accommodates a broad range of policy positions, and its persistent utility and ubiquity speak volumes. Indeed, blame is the central rationale of federal education policy as we know it.[16] Accountability, the idea that the successes and—much more importantly—failures of the nation's public schools can be placed squarely and without qualification on the shoulders of local educational professionals, is blame enthroned as policy. As a rhetorical strategy, blame also gives accountability the urgency of "an onrushing freight train," and its capacity to confer such urgency is part of why it has been such a popular appeal in the pursuit of reform.[17]

To account for the central role of blame in the discourse of education policy, I examine five of the most prominent cases of public persuasion over education policy since the founding of the ED, not only in terms of their intricacies as public acts, but also as strategic manipulations of their varying institutional contexts. This means shifting the frame of education policy scholarship from a point of view that prioritizes the parsing of successful and failed reform efforts to a broader concern with the shape and influence of those efforts that made the most substantial bids to write and rewrite the blame narrative that is the center of education policy making. Toward those ends, this book concerns education policy as an always-evolving national conversation instead of as a series of legislative decisions or the expression of structural forces. To wit, what follows is not a political or social history of education, but a "rhetorical history," an account of a few decades in the process of the mutual transformation Bailyn described.[18]

A BRIEF INTELLECTUAL HISTORY OF THE PUBLIC LIFE OF BLAME

A common complaint among educators, and fairly so, is that everyone believes him or herself an expert on the subject of education. It takes thirteen years of formal schooling just to earn a high school diploma. Americans commonly spend more than a decade and a half as students before leaving school behind and entering the workforce. As a result, it is not terribly surprising that many Americans feel they know a thing or two about education by the time they are finished with school, even if they had no formal training in education as a subject. Blame is similar. The Western intellectual tradition has been investigating the nature of blame in systematic philosophical treatises since ancient Athens. Humanity has had Aristotle's thoughts on blame for almost half a millennium longer than it has had Jesus's. Although only a small group of people are familiar with the breadth of the resulting tradition of philosophical and rhetorical inquiry, practically everyone on Earth has been coping with blame on a daily basis since birth. If experience is the best teacher, then all of humanity holds advanced degrees in both blame and education. But despite our ease and familiarity with blame, careful analysis reveals blaming as an intricate rhetorical act. As a result, blame has already received enough careful analysis to provide some initial trajectories for investigating its public life.

Two secular, intellectual traditions—philosophy and rhetoric—have theorized blame. In the middle of the twentieth century, blame came to play an integral role in one of the leading debates in philosophy. On one side, philosophers argued in favor of the existence of free will, whereas on the other side, philosophers argued—or at least feared—that free will is a particularly cruel illusion in a universe that is actually deterministic. In an essay that continues to be an early touchstone in that debate, British philosopher P. F. Strawson argued that blame can exist only in a world with free will. This, he posed, is because you must attribute to the person you are blaming the ability to have acted otherwise. If that person could not have acted otherwise—that is, the person's actions were predetermined by a universe that accords each person an inescapable future—then circumstance is responsible instead of the accused. Strawson thus postulated that blaming is not just an attribution of fault, but also a complementary attribution of agency.[19] For example, Strawson's observation is inhered in David Tyack and Larry Cuban's often-cited observation: "Schools can easily shift from panacea to scapegoat."[20] Common to both roles is the power to make a difference: the attribution of agency.

By comparison, rhetoricians have been theorizing blame as strategic communication since the middle of the fourth century BCE. In *On Rhetoric*, Aristotle identified blame, *psogos*, as the opposite of praise, *epainos*. Together, praise and blame were the two halves of ceremonial, or *epideictic*, speaking. Epideictic oratory typically occurs during a ceremony like a wedding, graduation, or inauguration, and according to Aristotle, it celebrates a socially held value.[21] As strategic communication, epideictic rhetoric can be used to praise someone for upholding a value or to blame that same someone for violating it. Aristotle's rhetorical conception of blame is useful because it frees blame (along with praise) from the logical rigidity of the philosophical perspective on blame in favor of its *telos*, or ends. In this way, a rhetorical perspective privileges blame's use value as a social practice. For Aristotle, to blame is to speak negatively about another, regardless of whether any discrete fault is proven. There is an "I know it when I see it" element to Aristotle's description of blame, which is important to capture with a concept that everyone knows so intimately. Like Aristotle, we know disparaging speech when we encounter it, and this broad view of blame helps consolidate the past three and a half decades of education reform rhetoric. This big-tent conception of blame also connects the rhetoric of education with larger trends in political speech.

Aside from freeing blame of purely analytic moorings, understanding blame as strategic communication also aids in the analysis of blame as a public act. Kenneth Burke, a twentieth-century American public intellectual, offered another helpful perspective; he described blame as a societal ritual of purification. To blame, according to Burke, one must identify a scapegoat, load a collection of social ills onto that scapegoat, ritualistically banish the scapegoat, and then reunite a newly purified society without the scapegoated entity and the ills it had come to embody.[22] Burke's ritualistic description of blame has been used as the basis for social scientific inquiry, but I will not try to describe and then demonstrate the existence of a series of steps universal to the rhetoric of school reform. Instead, I want to draw attention to Burke's keen sense of audience. Blaming in public is not done for the sake of the blamed, or the "scapegoated," as Burke would have it. In fact, the accused are typically a means, not an end, for blaming. Thus, as a tool for influencing public policy, blame is not committed for the person or persons being blamed, but for some larger audience who is persuaded by witnessing blame.

I call this politically calculated performance of accusation undertaken as a means of persuasion "public blame." I append *public* to indicate a concern with what blame accomplishes as popular, civic discourse—that is, how blame, through its circulation, calls people together to take collective action.[23] This means addressing empirical examples of blame as they are employed to influence the world of human affairs. This distinction is important because most of the contemporary philosophical study of blame concerns blame in the form of hypothetical cases.[24] Although the intricacy and justice of blame, especially interpersonal blame, can be elegantly unfolded in a philosophical vacuum, that unfolding holds static the probabilistic elements that make blaming both spectacular and political as public speech. Blame deployed in the course of the public discussion of education policy is not hypothetical, but empirical. It is blame out in the world engaged in the messy process of influencing human affairs. Unlike private or interpersonal blame, public blame is not defined by its *perfection* of justice, but by its *presentation* of justice. In this way, public blame is always a political act loosed into a discursive context already swimming with rival acts of blame. The comparison of these competing and public acts of blame organizes and directs my analysis. To compare them, I draw on Burke, Aristotle, Strawson, and a rotating cast of scholars who have written about the nature of blame, rhetoric, and policy making. I also break down public bllame into a rhetorical act with three critical elements, each of which serves as an entry point for critical inquiry.

First, public blame is a political animal. It is a persuasive performance fashioned for the benefit of a strategically selected audience. That audience usually has some sought-after political power and, perhaps as a consequence, is typically invited to join in blaming someone or something else. Importantly, the target audience for public blame is only rarely the blamed themselves. For example, when a politician or policy advocate declares the public schools are to blame for failing America's children, he or she might reasonably hope that such an accusation might convince parents, citizens, or elected officials to support some policy or candidacy. However, such an accusation will probably not get the people who collectively make up the public schools to acquiesce to their supposed culpability. In response to blame, the blamed party might issue a rebuttal, but the blamer's goal is to exert influence over the target audience, not those who are blamed.[25] For the accuser, the accused are a rhetorical prop. The blamed party's response, the accuracy or fairness of the accusation, and the consequence of the accusation for those blamed are largely beside the point.

Second, public blame traffics in agency. Because public blame has a deliberative purpose, it seeks the assent of the public on not just the fault of the accused, but also the implications of that fault. For Strawson, blaming says as much about what the accuser thinks about the way the world works as it does about what the accuser thinks about the accused. Public blame is similar. It foregrounds certain causal relationships and backgrounds others, creating a landscape of action and consequence onto which certain policy decisions can be successfully projected and others cannot. If the public schools are solely responsible for educational failure, and educational failure is defined as declining test scores, then policies targeting children's home lives or art education are largely irrelevant to school reform. Public blame thereby creates a loaded context for judgment. This context is not usually as polarized as the diametric choice between determinism and free will, but successful blame narratives articulate assumptions about race, economics, gender, and other categories of social analysis, causally relating those categories to academic achievement and other education policy goals. Looking at blame in the context of education policy offers an opportunity to improve the understanding of how acts of blame fit their social context and how they try to exert pressure on that context, especially as they rearrange the power to act. That is, as they rearrange agency.

Third, public blame is ethical. In one sense, to blame is to enact ethical judgment.[26] When a policy advocate blames in public, he or she assigns culpability to someone or something for some public problem. Such an accusation must be grounded, explicitly or implicitly, in a set of expectations for ethical action that the accused has presumably violated. For example, if an education reformer accuses public school officials of failing American students as evidenced by low test scores, that reformer must rely on members of the target audience recognizing bad test scores as evidence of educational malfeasance, perhaps a failure of due diligence. This ethical dimension to blaming—as well as praising—is why Aristotle identified the celebration of a socially held value as the rhetorical purpose of epideictic oratory. This social dimension is critical for blame in the context of public advocacy. As policy advocates attribute fault to the person or persons being blamed, they simultaneously attribute their expectations for ethical action to their audience, the target of public blame's persuasion. Thus, through public blame, policy advocates align themselves ethically with their audience, laying the foundations for a coalition of conscience.

However, public blame is ethical in yet another sense. Public blame expresses a set of ethical expectations for others, but must also live up to the ethical expectations others have for it. As a persuasive strategy carried out through public discourse, public blame affects the quality of our civic life in a paradoxical manner. Public blame can be a courageous act of civic faith calling fellow citizens to action by appealing to a shared judgment as well as a shared belief in the justness of democratic change. However, when it is perceived as disingenuous, public blame can erode the prospects for shared judgment and democratic change. When public blame becomes ubiquitous, perfunctory, or detached from the bounds of good taste by the gamesmanship of mass persuasion, it not only fails to persuade, but also undermines the democratic culture it relies upon to make change in the world. We call such failed attempts at public blame "passing the buck," "throwing under the bus," "ratting out," and so forth. And, when we sense we have seen too many of them, we throw up our hands. These abuses of blame damage the reputations of public blame and those who commit it. But unfortunately, they also damage the reputation of political dialogue itself. Over time, our public discourse can lose its vitality, integrity, and sophistication if it devolves into a blame game. In this way, blaming has consequences for the entire discussion of education policy.

This brings me to a brief, but important disclaimer. More often than not, I argue in this book that blame is ill-advised or at cross-purposes with what I will defend as reasonable expectations for the quality of civic speech. Despite my concerns, I will not argue that blame, even in the form of public blame, is inherently bad. I also will not argue that public blame should be eliminated. Indeed, I will partake in plenty of public blaming, and like the advocates in the case studies I examine, I hope to use blame to persuade a target audience of scholars and education professionals to agree with me. Still, my primary goal throughout this book is to reveal how public blame pursues and, from time to time, achieves persuasion in the discourse of education policy. By peering behind blame's public façade, I hope readers will take away a broadened and empowered understanding of the rhetoric of policy advocacy. I also hope to encourage if not fewer, then more thoughtful acts of public blame. So, although this is a book about education policy as sophistry, it is neither a model of blameless public argument nor a defense of reckless speech. I believe there is a broad and accommodating middle road of responsible public dialogue between those two extremes, a path I both implicitly advocate and explicitly seek to inhabit in these pages.

DISSOI PSOGOI: FIVE CASE STUDIES AND ONE PARADOX IN THE RHETORIC OF EDUCATION POLICY

The sophists were the pre-Socratic rhetoricians of the ancient Greek world. They were also its teachers. Often competing with each other, the sophists wrote and delivered speeches in celebrated displays of public eloquence. They also taught Greek men of means the skills of public argument. The sophists made many important contributions to the intellectual history of public speech in the Western world, all before Plato coined the term *rhetoric*.[27] Among their contributions is the concept *dissoi logoi*, which translates to "opposing words." For the sophists, this was both an educational exercise and a belief. As an exercise, *dissoi logoi* amounted to an argument.[28] Those engaged in it would speak in opposition to each other, using words to oppose other words. As a concept, *dissoi logoi* signaled a belief held by the sophists that, in any given case, there are always words available to oppose those already spoken. In more familiar terms, the sophists believed that there is always room for debate. This belief in the immutability of opposing rhetorical action and the educational value of exploring the range of potential responses undergirds all rhetorical analysis.

Inspired by the sophistic tradition of public argument, this book is an investigation of *dissoi psogoi*, or "opposing blames." As a consequence, two mutually reinforcing purposes drove the selection of a series of representative episodes that tell this history of education reform. On the one hand, this study is a step toward the description of public blame as a diverse and consequential rhetorical form. In order to focus on blame as a rhetorical strategy that can be deployed in a number of ways to influence a particular policy process, confining the case studies to education holds that policy process somewhat static. Each of the instances of blaming that serves as a case study advances a particular education policy as a solution for the educational failures of the public schools. By exploring five case studies, all from the relatively recent history of education policy, this book compares how each policy advocate concocted his or her own kind of public blame in an effort to influence a policy process they all perceive themselves as sharing. Like the sophists who had faith in *dissoi logoi*, I believe that there is a rhetorical education to be had in an extended engagement with *dissoi psogoi*. In these cases, blame works in combination with other rhetorical forms: *ad hominem*, self-blame, metaphor, scapegoating, and confession. Together, the five case studies provide insight into a broad range of blame's rhetorical dimensions as public discourse.

Additionally, by selecting five case studies in the popular discourse of education policy since the founding of the ED, a particular kind of historical narrative emerges, a history of rhetorical practice. Federal education policy in the United States experienced dramatic change from 1980 to 2010. Education scholars have offered a range of explanations for how the federal role in public education suddenly expanded so much, and with the surprising support of political actors who typically oppose the expansion of federal power. Some researchers have attributed this change to overlapping interests among institutional policy entrepreneurs, others have identified colliding interests between large historical movements in education, another camp declared the dawning of a new political era in the early 1980s, and still others have constructed new models of political action such as the paradigm shift.[29] I point to a public conversation awash in blame and argue that the coalescence that took form in the early 1980s was not so much a commitment to any particular vision of America's educational future, but instead a consensus about a particular strategy used to argue for it. The era of accountability is more the product of the unanimity of public blame in the discourse of education reform than any consensus around how education ought to be governed.[30] To make this case, I examine five prominent acts of public blame from the 1980s through the 2000s, each in its own chapter.

From the 1980s, I examine two successful appeals for education reform: an hour of public television featuring the educational philosophy of Milton Friedman and the National Commission on Excellence in Education's (NCEE) influential report, *A Nation at Risk: The Imperative for Educational Reform*. As with all of the case studies, Friedman and the NCEE presented a compelling appeal for education reform by laying blame for the failures of US public education. In the Friedman chapter, I give his rhetorical success well-deserved attention by examining the deliberative consequences of directing blame at an other. Friedman's success as an advocate for school vouchers relied on his savvy decision to blame bureaucrats using their professional status as an *ad hominem*. Friedman characterized himself as a brave individual resisting the bureaucrats' collectivizing influence thereby modeling a political posture for disgruntled parents. In the NCEE chapter, I reconsider the widely acknowledged rhetorical success of *A Nation at Risk* by examining how the NCEE blamed the American people for the failures of public education. Capitalizing on their ability as fellow Americans to both place and accept blame, the report authors used self-directed blame to create a monologic appeal that appeared to be the product of a dialogue that did not happen. This rhetorical sleight of hand foreclosed the *stasis* of cause, propelling the public discourse of education toward new policy.

From the 1990s, I examine Jonathan Kozol's *Savage Inequalities: Children in America's Schools*. Despite its popularity and venerable argument, I judge Kozol's book a rhetorical failure. Accounting for the failures of public education by blaming environmental factors instead of people, *Savage Inequalities* succeeded at garnering a great deal of public attention, but deployed blame counterproductively to its policy goals. Taking issue with the nearly universal praise for *Savage Inequalities*, I compare the book's policy advocacy, desegregation, with its public reception as an impassioned appeal for funding reform.[31] To accomplish this assessment, I argue that Kozol's choice to write metaphorically about East St. Louis as a third world city contributed to a popular misreading of his book.

From the 2000s, I examine the No Child Left Behind Act of 2001 (NCLB) and the public scholarship of Diane Ravitch. Both cases direct blame at governmental systems. I argue that as NCLB legislated a federal system of standards-based accountability, it simultaneously instituted a preferred blame narrative for public education. By scapegoating street-level bureaucrats, the rhetoric of accountability serves the interests of legislators, removing responsibility for the success and failure of public education from lawmakers and placing it on educational professionals. In its attempt to provide an official answer to the question of who or what is to blame for the purported failures of US public education, NCLB opened a discussion about systems of governance as the critical problem, laying the foundation for itself to become the target of blame for those same failures.[32]

To explore the blaming of NCLB, I follow the conversion of Diane Ravitch from a firm supporter of the law to one of its most vehement detractors. In her op-eds, blog posts, and books on the subject, Ravitch gave voice to white, working-class discomfort with the desegregation by category created when NCLB lumped many rural and suburban schools together with inner-city schools as failing. In the popular critiques to which Ravitch lends her support, such as the narrowing of curricula and the inability of standardized testing to quantify the nuances of good schooling, I find Ravitch reiterating an apprehension with the deceptive nature of NCLB. Reframed as such, Ravitch succeeded at both blaming NCLB for the educational failures of the 2000s and excusing her support for it during that same time.

Across five episodes over three decades, a remarkably stable consensus emerges in the supposedly contentious politics of public education. Nearly everyone agrees that the US public school system is failing to live up to expectations. This broad consensus makes fertile ground for the laying of blame, a rhetorical form that continuously reenergizes the pursuit of education reform. As scholars reconsider the wisdom of perpetual education reform, they must also reconsider the wisdom of unending blame, reform's discursive fountain of youth. To imagine a different educational future, we must ask how it is we have been imagining the educational past throughout the era of achievement. Thus, in two final synthesis chapters, I consider the paradox of public blame—that blame both calls upon and undermines our civic faith. In the first such chapter, I consider how the ubiquity of blame in the discourse of education policy has helped create an era of accountability in education policy and how that era now threatens the publicness of schooling. Then, in the second synthesis chapter, I consider alternatives to the contemporary overreliance on public blame, such as blaming less frequently, using praise, and developing an interpretive tradition that attends to the rhetoric of education reform.

1

Milton Friedman Blames the Bureaucrats

In 1980, with Jimmy Carter's Department of Education just a few months old, the Public Broadcasting Service (PBS) began airing a television series written and narrated by University of Chicago economist Milton Friedman.[1] Entitled *Free to Choose*, the series was composed of ten hour-long episodes, each delivering a brief, entertaining economics lesson. Bringing big ideas to the small screen, the series mixed public scholarship, investigative journalism, and public debate into persuasive appeals for the free-market policies Friedman had championed as a professor at Chicago. More than just a television program, *Free to Choose* included an eponymous book coauthored by Friedman with his wife Rose, herself a professor of law at Chicago. In order to maximize the educational impact of *Free to Choose*, the Friedmans' book was organized into chapters corresponding to each of the show's episodes replete with explanations and examples.

By combining public television and best-selling nonfiction, Friedman made *Free to Choose* his multimedia manifesto proclaiming the virtues of neoliberal economic policy.[2] He also made *Free to Choose* nearly identical to *The Age of Uncertainty*, a British Broadcasting Corporation miniseries with its own book and famous economist. Written and narrated by Harvard University's John Kenneth Galbraith, *The Age of Uncertainty* took to the air three years before *Free to Choose* and culminated in Galbraith's call for a "new socialism."[3] *Free to Choose* was Friedman's public response to his midcentury rival in a battle for economic hearts and minds. In this effort to win a privatized future, nine of the show's ten episodes featured Friedman's thoughts on traditional economic policy controversies such as the proper role of government in regulating welfare, inflation, and taxes. Altogether, Friedman's show and book advanced a stern but energetic counterpoint to Galbraith's show and book. However, the sixth installment of *Free to Choose* stood somewhat apart from the rest of the economic fracas.

Entitled "What's Wrong with Our Schools?" episode six featured Friedman making his case for public school vouchers as a solution for sagging test scores, miscreant students, and ballooning bureaucracy. Deftly folding his economic ideas into a national conversation already exasperated about declining test scores and urban decay, Friedman advocated the creation of an educational marketplace through the reallocation of public funds from a direct-to-schools model to parent-controlled vouchers. He argued that competition among schools for voucher funds would give parents more choice in where they could send their children to school and improve the overall quality of elementary and secondary education in the United States. Although Friedman developed his vision of an educational marketplace long before the advent of the Department of Education (ED), the federalization of education policy brought on by the new department made it possible to imagine the implementation of vouchers as a uniform, national policy.

Unlike the reestablished ED, the debate over school vouchers was not new in 1980, not for the US public and certainly not for Friedman. The seventh chapter of his most popular scholarly book, *Capitalism and Freedom*, was entitled "The Role of Government in Education" and helped garner some attention for school vouchers in 1962, but Friedman first published his thoughts on school vouchers in a chapter he contributed to an essay collection made in tribute to the late Columbia University economics professor Eugene Agger in 1955.[4] In fact, Friedman is typically credited—perhaps more often blamed—for beginning the public discussion over school vouchers.[5] However, both of Friedman's early writings argued for school vouchers on the grounds that they would break up an inefficient state monopoly while preserving society's interest in a well-educated citizenry. Although written in a lively academic style, Friedman's scholarly essays stuck to the economic case for vouchers. Neither engaged in any overt blaming. That changed, however, when Friedman took to the airwaves. Unlike his academic writing on the subject, Friedman's televisual case for vouchers made extensive use of blame. "What's Wrong with Our Schools?" asked episode six. "Bureaucrats," responded Friedman.

As I work through Friedman's persuasive appeal in the televised version of "What's Wrong with Our Schools?" I resort frequently to the pause button. Taking it slow, I try to diagram Friedman's rhetorical dance steps as he used blame to remake his case for school vouchers so that it would appeal to the PBS-watching public. In particular, I explore how the two segments of "What's Wrong with Our Schools?" (described more fully below) blamed in different, but complementary, ways. The first segment, a newsmagazine-style report on the condition of the US public schools, followed Friedman around the country as he portrayed public educators, especially public school administrators, as an oppressive bureaucracy ruining the public schools. Talking on a stool outside a one-room schoolhouse, in front of a fleet of school buses, and from a lounge chair in Dartmouth's Sanborn Library, Friedman spoke frankly with his viewing public. According to Friedman, educational bureaucrats were bent on protecting their own interests and had been doing so at the expense of parents and students. The second segment, a public debate between Friedman and four prominent education experts, Albert Shanker, Gregory Anrig, Thomas Shannon, and Thomas Coons, saw Friedman labeling his opponents "bureaucrats." Implicitly, this made them responsible for the decline of public education detailed in the first half of the episode. Explicitly, Friedman argued that their professional identity predisposed them to an ideological bias that inhibited not just their ability to do their jobs well, but their ability to make credible contributions to the debate with Friedman. In Friedman's remarkably persuasive, two-pronged act of public blaming, I uncover a sly form of *ad hominem—ad bureaucratem*—a rhetorical maneuver that has influenced the public discussion of education policy ever since.

PUBLIC BLAME AND *AD HOMINEM*

To use blame in public discourse, one must make a number of strategic decisions, not the least of which is *whom* to blame. Presumably this decision is simplified by a genuine belief in the guilt of the accused, but regardless of the sincerity of any given accusation, blaming before an audience entails some degree of strategic calculation. For example, before blaming it is wise to consider the feasibility of any potential accusation by at least asking, Who will believe me? When a team of people write a book or produce a television series—or in this case both—the opportunities for conversation and reflection about the strategic aspects of blaming are manifold. Consequently, this chapter treats "What's Wrong with Our Schools?" as a persuasive appeal that, regardless of its authors' intentions, was thoughtfully designed and could have been different.

In "What's Wrong with Our Schools?" Friedman first blamed bureaucrats in the abstract as an absent category of ne'er-do-wells ruining public education, but when the episode transferred from a field report to a public debate, Friedman blamed bureaucrats sitting across from him in the same room. The spectacular result of this blaming strategy was that Friedman appeared to decisively win the public debate portion of the show despite taking on four opponents all by himself. However, Friedman's use of blame in the public debate became the familiar logical fallacy, *ad hominem*. Friedman attacked the character of his opponents, indicting them on the grounds of their shared professional identity. This use of blame undermined the fairness and ultimately the legitimacy of the deliberation, but it also demonstrated the effectiveness of blame in deliberations over education policy because, to the untrained eye, it worked.

The systematic study of logical fallacies stretches all the way back to Aristotle's short treatise, *Sophistical Refutations*, where he described categories of arguments that appear sound but, upon closer inspection, are not.[6] For Aristotle, fallacies grow out of the space between reality and its representation in language. As the Latin term implies, *ad hominem* was not included in the surviving text of Aristotle's original list of fallacies from ancient Athens. Nonetheless, contemporary scholarship has determined that the faulty logic *ad hominem* describes dates back to Aristotle. *Ad hominem* literally means "to the person," and it refers to a category of arguments that respond by attacking the other speaker, usually along moral or ethical lines.[7] *Argumentum ad hominem* is considered a fallacy when it dismisses the content of an argument on the grounds that the person who made the argument deserves disregard. Thus an *ad hominem* makes the faulty assumption that a bad person cannot make a good argument. *Ad hominem* is not considered a fallacy when the character of the person it attacks is relevant to the argument at hand. Someone's past moral behavior certainly is germane to whether or not that person is likely to behave morally in the future, a reasonable consideration in an election, for example. Philosopher Henry Johnstone observed that all valid philosophical argument is *ad hominem* in the sense that all arguments that invoke principles are person-directed.[8] Nonetheless, there is a category of *ad hominem* that is unfair to the accused in such a way that its use corrodes the quality of public discourse, and that is the kind of *ad hominem* this analysis concerns.

Recently, *ad hominem* has been the subject of a surge of empirical research concerned with how the form works in public argument. Katarzyna Budzynska and Maciej Witek have found that *ad hominem* relies on the ethos of the speaker in order to persuade.[9] That is, whoever wishes to use *ad hominem* persuasively must have a strong character, or ethos, in the eyes of his or her audience. I agree with their findings and will show that *ad hominem* in "What's Wrong with Our Schools?" does indeed rely upon Friedman's ethos, but I add that *ad hominem* also helped him build his ethos by creating the appearance of virtuosic debating. Bart Garssen has found that *ad hominem*, despite being despised as rude and illogical, often goes undetected. This is because it takes on the appearance of a reasoned response when it is positioned as a rejoinder to an argument from authority. The way "What's Wrong with Our Schools?" first shows Friedman attacking an absent and supposedly authoritative bureaucracy before transforming that blame narrative into a full-frontal *ad hominem* during the public debate fits Garssen's observation exactly. Audrey Yap has found that *ad hominem* is effective even when the irrelevance of the accusation is recognized, a finding that supports the wisdom, if not the ethics, of Friedman's argumentative strategy.[10]

To these helpful findings, I layer an additional dimension. *Ad hominem* in the midst of deliberation aspires to silence others.[11] In the introduction, I discussed how P. F. Strawson observed that blame gives agency to the person who is blamed by crediting that person with the capacity to do whatever bad thing he or she is accused of as well as the ability to have chosen not to do that bad thing. Just as blame credits the accused party with the agency to make change out in the world, in the context of a deliberation, it subtracts the agency to speak about the world in a reliable way. *Ad hominem*, as a kind of blame, attempts to obliterate a speaker's ethos. Given full weight, an *ad hominem* argument would rule the contributions of the accused out of the deliberation. Blame in the form of *ad hominem* thus provides an argumentative tool that threatens the fairness and integrity of a deliberation, a concerning outcome when public conversation is the genesis of future policy making.

AD BUREAUCRATEM

Writing for the *St. Croix Review* in 1999, Friedman shared the political philosophy underlying his vision for America's educational future. "In an ideal world," he declared, "the state would play no role in education."[12] Presented in Friedman's characteristically direct style, this straightforward declaration belies its radicalism. Public education is a humongous government enterprise arguably constituting the biggest, most expansive, and longest-running social welfare program ever undertaken in the United States.[13] Historically, the states have borne the greatest burden in administering and paying for public education. But, even as the federal government began taking a greater role in funding and directing public education during the second half of the twentieth century, education continues to strain state budgets.[14] Friedman's preference for a government-free education system cuts against this long-standing commitment on the part of state governments as well as the trend toward increasingly interventionist policy on the part of the federal government. Nonetheless, over the scant sixty minutes that constitute "What's Wrong with Our Schools?" Friedman manages to make a radical privatization agenda seem not just moderate, but natural—a commonsense response to the dire problems facing public education in the United States. To achieve this impressive feat of popular persuasion, Friedman capitalizes on the then emerging consensus that America's public schools were failing their educational mission, especially in urban areas.[15]

"What's Wrong with Our Schools?" consists of two half-hour segments. The first presents Friedman alone making his case against bureaucracy, and the second features a debate between Friedman and four education experts. The first half is a fast-paced study in contrasts, making the extent of Friedman's blaming easy to miss. Over thirty minutes, Friedman introduces his audience to a diverse collection schools: rich and poor; urban, rural, and suburban; public and private; parochial and charter; primary, secondary, and collegiate. The schools represent a broad range of socioeconomic contexts and administrative structures. As Friedman speaks either on location or over images of each of his many example institutions, their differences help facilitate his act of public blaming. Generalizing from his cases, Friedman insists that good schools are clean, parent-run, and independent from centralization—preferably private. Bad schools, by comparison, are neglectful of their facilities, scornful of parental concerns, and beholden to a centralized state bureaucracy. Friedman unabashedly commends and condemns his example schools throughout the segment, pointing to scene and after scene of scholastic failure coinciding with bureaucracy.

Friedman initiates his case at the very beginning of "What's Wrong with Our Schools?" After a lead-in montage of Friedman portraiture set to an uplifting orchestral theme song, the episode opens with footage of students arriving at Boston's Hyde Park High School. As the mostly black students pass through metal detectors on their way into the school, Friedman uses vivid language to describe the scene. Students are "faced by security guards looking for hidden weapons" and "watched over by armed police." As one student submits to a frisking that looks revealingly casual, Friedman's disembodied voice rightly laments Hyde Park's correctional atmosphere. "Isn't that awful?" he asks in a disappointed tone. "What can be learned under these circumstances?" Shot in the morning on a typical school day, the scenes from Hyde Park depict the drudgery of the morning routine at a school in a struggling urban community. Although a dearth of enthusiastic scholasticism in the early morning of an average weekday might be understandable at any school, Friedman's narration enlists the banality of the scene in his budding diatribe against bureaucracy. According to the still visually-absent Friedman, Hyde Park is a bad school providing an education that is both expensive and joyless to students who have no better option. Worse still, insists Friedman, Hyde Park is "a vivid illustration of the problems facing America's schools."[16]

From the bustle of urban Boston, "What's Wrong with Our Schools?" cuts to the tranquility of rural Vermont. Sitting on a desk outside "the last one-room schoolhouse" in the state, the now-present Friedman gives his version of America's recent educational history. Over a soundtrack of persistent bird chirping, Friedman recalls "the way it used to be," when parents controlled their children's schools. According to Friedman, the history of public education is a cautionary tale of government run amok. Parents used to be the ones "choosing the teacher," "monitoring the schooling," and "even getting together and chipping in to paint the schoolhouse." "Increasingly," Friedman laments, "schools have come under the control of centralized administration." Friedman builds his argument by contrasting the "slums of the big cities" with "bucolic Vermont." At bad schools, bureaucrats are in charge. At good ones, parents are. In school districts like Boston, "professional educators" decide "what shall be taught, who shall do the teaching, and even what children shall go to what school."[17] On location in Vermont, Friedman delivers his history lesson in the utter tranquility of a midsummer day. No students or security guards intrude on the carefully chosen scene where he sits alone. The result is a contrast in location as sharp as the contrast in Friedman's argument. Whereas contemporary public education in Boston is a nightmare of grinding bureaucracy, the last vestige of America's educational yesteryear is a place of genteel contemplation. The result is an aesthetic contrast between good and bad education as sharp as Friedman's words.

Cutting again to another location, Friedman continues his narration over establishing shots of the Weston High School band performing *Pomp and Circumstance*.[18] As pairs of white students walk side-by-side in two gender-segregated lines to Elgar's graduation march, Friedman explains that their "well-off" parents have used their affluence to move to "one of Boston's wealthier suburbs." Friedman then invites his audience to recall the contrast between Boston and Vermont. Because their school is public, the parents at Weston High School "pay taxes instead of tuition," but they "get better value for their money than do the parents at Hyde Park." Friedman then explains that, "because they've kept a good deal of control over the local schools," the Weston High parents have "managed to retain many of the virtues of the one-room schoolhouse." Friedman never discusses the pitfalls of local control, problems that are at least gently implied by Stepford students marching in a rigidly choreographed graduation ritual at Weston, but he also only glosses the virtues of local control. He does not discuss the usual points of comparison like the breadth and depth of Weston's curriculum versus Hyde Park's or their graduation and college attendance rates. Although that information would presumably support his assessment, Friedman chooses to make his argument to a broad public on aesthetic grounds. Weston High's students wear white suits and dresses adorned with red corsages as they advance toward their undoubtedly promising futures, whereas Hyde Park's students arrive at school through metal detectors in a macabre rehearsal of their imperiled fates. Vermont is tranquil and friendly, whereas Boston is noisy and anonymous. In short, Weston High and the last one-room classroom in Vermont are prettier, wealthier, and whiter than Hyde Park, and all of these aesthetic qualities are proof in themselves of a higher quality of education. Although the contrast between a graduation ceremony and an average morning is unfairly calculated for maximum contrast—for all we know, Hyde Park's graduation is a blast—Friedman's aesthetic distinction is believable and dramatic.

By the end of these three scenes, Friedman has rearticulated the rise of educational bureaucracy—a complicated social and institutional history—as a power grab by bureaucrats.[19] He has encouraged his audience to associate the aesthetics of poverty and educational failure with strong government involvement in education. He has also encouraged his audience to view bureaucrats suspiciously as harboring selfish intentions. In short, Friedman's viewing public is primed for the persuasive appeal of public blame.

To ensure that his observations about Vermont and Boston will support his voucher advocacy, Friedman does not just associate bureaucrats with the failures of America's education system; he outright blames bureaucrats for those failures. Friedman is adamant—bureaucrats are the source of the problem. During the first half of "What's Wrong with Our Schools?" Friedman's accusation is pure public blame. He never speaks directly to any of the purportedly culpable bureaucrats during this segment. The only audience for his public act of blaming is the viewers at home. Wisely, then, Friedman rationalizes his act of blame by pitting bureaucrats and parents against each other in a struggle for the agency to control public education. According to Friedman, school administration is a zero-sum game. Any decision made by a bureaucrat is a decision that could have been made by a parent or group of parents. From this point of view, bureaucrats are the natural enemies of parents and educational bureaucracy itself is a perversion of parental agency. Friedman also flatters his audience by making them the heroes in his history of American education. Of course, if parents are heroes, then bureaucrats are villains, and villains make for good TV.

Leaving New England behind, "What's Wrong with Our Schools?" cuts to old England to offer a representative anecdote of malicious bureaucracy.[20] Dennis Gee, the balding headmaster of the Newtown Primary School in the sleepy English town of Ashford, plays the part of villain superbly. Headmaster Gee and parent Maurice Walton trade camera time as they present opposing views on a proposed school voucher program. As the episode tacks between the increasingly stern interlocutors, Friedman's voice periodically interjects, guiding the audience's interpretation of their dispute.

Gee, who would be at home in a Monty Python skit about the eccentricities of British bureaucracy, makes no secret of his disdain for vouchers and the parents who would like to use them. He refers to the voucher as a "sticky little piece of paper" and bemoans the agency that a voucher system would give to parents. "We see this as a barrier between us and the parents," he explains. Gee worries aloud about voucher-wielding parents "coming in" to the school "and under duress" commanding teachers, "'You will do this or else!'"[21] For Gee just as for Friedman, parental decision making trades off with professional expertise. Above all else, Gee fears that vouchers will give parents the power to force educators to make decisions against their professional judgment. The headstrong headmaster makes Friedman's argument for him, demonstrating in his words and actions that agency over a child's education is a zero-sum game. Later, when Friedman turns to advocate vouchers in the debate portion of the show, this contest over agency becomes crucial because it pits parents and educators against each other. If agency over education really is a zero-sum game, then the only way for parents to empower themselves is to take decision-making power away from bureaucrats.

Gee's statements are helpful for Friedman's case not just because of their contentious content, but also because of their acrimonious tone. As the scene in Ashford begins to cut back and forth between the headmaster and the parent, Gee's imperiousness justifies an outraged response from Mr. Walton. With palpable discontent, Mr. Walton expresses his desire to use vouchers to force teachers to "pull their socks up and give us a better deal." Although the campaign for vouchers is the argument against the status quo to which Gee is responding, "What's Wrong with Our Schools?" arranges the interaction in the reverse: Gee speaks first and Mr. Walton responds. So, when Mr. Walton talks about teachers having "a gun at the parent's head" and then declares that he would like to reverse the situation, his argument is contextualized as responsive instead of aggressive. Arranging Mr. Walton's comments as a reaction to Gee's reasserts the blameworthiness of bureaucrats by situating them as the aggressors. Lest the guilt of treating educational professionals unfairly get the better of any audience members, Mr. Walton offers absolution. Considering aloud the power a voucher system would give parents over teachers, Mr. Walton confesses that he "can only say tough on the teachers."[22] By this point in Friedman's report the gloves are off; parents and educators are unapologetically fighting with each other for control of the schools.

Friedman capitalizes on this local dispute between a bureaucrat and a parent using the headmaster's vague language to expand the conflict well beyond its Kentish context. Gee expresses his concerns about vouchers as a collective opposition. "It's this sort of philosophy of the marketplace that we object to," he explains.[23] Speaking in response to some off-camera prompting, the headmaster never contextualizes his "we." Gee might be invoking the membership of the local teachers union where, Friedman is quick to point out, he serves as secretary. Gee might have the administration and/or teachers of Newtown Primary School in mind when he says "we." Whatever group Gee meant to enlist, Friedman, as narrator, ensures that "we" reinforces a universal opposition between bureaucrats and parents. Rephrasing Gee's words, Friedman treats the headmaster as a spokesperson for educational bureaucrats everywhere: "In other words, Mr. Gee objects to giving the customer, in this case the parent, anything to say about the kind of schooling his child gets. Instead, the bureaucrats should decide."[24] When Friedman rearticulates Gee, any markers of local context, save the headmaster's name, are eliminated. Parents in Freidman's audience are invited to read themselves into this conflict between an imperious British headmaster and a disgruntled parent. Moreover, Friedman leaves "parent" singular, but makes "bureaucrats" plural. Not only are parents invited to think of themselves as part of a conflict; they are invited to read themselves into an asymmetrical conflict. Each parent struggles in singularity against the plural bureaucrats, a subtle but important distinction Friedman will use to his advantage during the debate.

According to Friedman, the conflict between parents and bureaucrats was not simply a struggle for control, it was an extension of his own ideological struggle with Galbraith. Tellingly, Friedman never again returns to the idea of vouchers in the rest of the first half of the episode. Instead of contesting the question of vouchers, a move that would risk outing his rhetorical strategy, "What's Wrong with Our Schools?" works instead to align parents by their economic interests on the side of neoliberalism and privatization, and bureaucrats by their professional interests in favor of socialism and centralization. To support his policy argument, Friedman needed more than a contest over agency for agency's sake, but less than a direct advocacy of school vouchers. Instead, Friedman needed to substantiate his act of blaming with a causal relationship between bureaucracy and educational failure. He had to establish the culpability of bureaucrats, and for that he needed some account of their motivations and intent. Moreover, this account had to implicate the bureaucrats' will to control public education without simultaneously incriminating parents for pursuing the same interest.

Blame's capacity to arrange agency proved critical for Friedman's rhetoric. Throughout the first half of "What's Wrong with Our Schools?" Friedman lauds the virtues of individual agency and decries the evils of collective agency. Each stop on his tour of US public schools was an opportunity to reinforce this position. For example, Friedman describes Saint John Chrysostom School in the South Bronx as "a joy to visit," noting that the parents have "picked this school" for their children and that they "are paying some of the costs from their own pockets."[25] Even though the school serves poor parents in a poor neighborhood, Friedman argues that their wealth of individual agency ensures a quality educational experience. Friedman's use of agency to account for educational success and failure in the context of Saint John Chrysostom rationalizes the school's unlikely success as it implicitly rebuts competing explanations like socioeconomic status or selectivity. Saint John Chrysostom serves as proof that individual agency is the crucial ingredient.

Turning his attention to higher education, Friedman contrasts Dartmouth College and the University of California, Los Angeles (UCLA). Yet again, Friedman employs individual agency to call attention to the differences between the two schools and to demonstrate the superiority of Dartmouth, an elite private institution. At Dartmouth, Friedman finds students hard at work serving patrons in the school's hotel and managing a call center that solicits alumni donations. As Friedman speaks from a chair in the well-attended and well-appointed Sanborn Library, he observes that "the real value of education is brought home" at Dartmouth.[26] The high cost of a Dartmouth education, Friedman reasons, requires an equally high level of buy-in from Ivy League students and parents. Compared to Dartmouth, the UCLA Bruins fare quite poorly. Unlike Dartmouth's industrious student body, UCLA students are depicted as lazy and directionless. Whereas each of the Dartmouth students' productive activities is given camera time with an accompanying interview, none of the UCLA students are given the opportunity to address Friedman's audience. Additionally, Friedman narrates his analysis of UCLA over a prolonged shot of young people recreating at what is presumably the school's outdoor pool, a dramatic contrast with the staid studiousness inside Sanborn.

Like the Saint John Chrysostom example, the excess of individual agency brought about by high tuition at Dartmouth is presented as proof that individual agency is the crucial determinant of educational success. From Friedman's point of view, UCLA's state-subsidized schooling creates a "distortion" in the "education marketplace."[27] UCLA shelters its students from the true monetary value of their education, robbing them of the motivation they need to invest properly in its pursuit. Attributing Dartmouth's relative success versus UCLA's to the influence of state support ignores some compelling alternative explanations for Dartmouth's educational achievements—like its more than two centuries of institutional momentum, the selectivity of its admissions process, and its impressively small class sizes.

Nonetheless, Friedman's take on university education provides a theory of motive that values individual agency over collective agency. Economic incentives that are felt directly by an individual who then acts on his or her own behalf are the only trustworthy basis for good educational policy making in Friedman's neoliberal view.[28] Bureaucrats, due to their collectivizing nature, cannot foster, and in fact disrupt, meaningful individual agency. For example, when Friedman tells the story of Harlem Preparatory Academy, a "storefront school" set up to help struggling New York students, he stresses the purported ill effects of bureaucratic oversight. According to Friedman, the students make "a deliberate choice to come to Harlem Prep" and thereby find "the teaching they want." Although the teachers do not have the certification "papers" required by the state, "that has not stopped them from doing a good job," lectures Friedman. As a consequence of its students' and teachers' exercise of individual agency, presumably channeling their economic motivations into their pursuit of quality education, Harlem Prep "was a very successful school." Friedman notes that "many students went on to college; some to leading colleges." However, all of this changed when "the school was taken over by bureaucrats."[29] Although the board of education was stepping in to keep the school from closing due to a budget crisis, they planned to move Harlem Prep to a traditional school building and bring the school under the oversight of the New York City Public Schools. The school board's takeover also coincided with the resignation of some thirty teachers and the school's principal. Framing the Harlem Prep example, Friedman observes that "the strangling of successful experiments by bureaucrats is not unusual." Here the influence of bureaucrats, even when they are offering aid, is depicted as blameworthy because bureaucratic action always collectivizes agency that would otherwise belong to individuals.

The first half of "What's Wrong with Our Schools?" ends with a benediction back in front of the first one-room schoolhouse in Vermont. "The system is not working!" Friedman declares. "It lacks a vital ingredient." According to Friedman, "A centralized system cannot possibly have that degree of personal concern for each individual child that we have as parents." In other words, the bureaucrats, by definition, collectivize what should be decision making driven by individual agents. For Friedman, the solution is obvious: "Market competition is the surest way to improve the quality and promote innovation in education as in every other field."[30] In Friedman's view, the flourishing of individual agency necessarily attends market competition, but that agency can only be gained by taking it from bureaucrats.

Altogether, Friedman's report creates a context for the following debate over school vouchers that heavily favors his position, both his policy advocacy and his debate performance. Although the debate in the second half of the episode concerns the viability of vouchers as a funding mechanism for improving US schools, the first segment makes very few direct arguments for Friedman's voucher solution. Indeed, Friedman's only extended discussion of vouchers emphasizes the intense opposition they encountered from Headmaster Gee. Nonetheless, Friedman's discussion of the virtues of individual agency enacted by parents and the evils of bureaucratic agency enacted by education professions both end up supporting his voucher advocacy, but not just by providing an ideological basis for his position. Friedman's report, airing before the debate, lays the groundwork for his *ad hominem* attack.

ARGUING WITH BUREAUCRATS

In contrast with the geographic expansiveness of the first half of "What's Wrong with Our Schools?" the second half never leaves one room in the Harper Memorial Library at the University of Chicago. In the North Reading Room, Friedman spars with four education experts: Albert Shanker, the president of the American Federation of Teachers; Thomas Shannon, the executive director of the National School Boards Association; Gregory Anrig, the commissioner of the Massachusetts Department of Education; and Thomas Coons, a law professor at the University of California, Berkeley, and the director of the Initiative for Family Choice in Education.[31] All four experts express reservations with Friedman's voucher advocacy, but Coons, unlike the other three, advocates a modified version of Friedman's voucher system. Robert McKenzie, a British elections expert and television personality, moderates the debate, using his position primarily to encourage the experts to clarify their opposition and keep all of the discussants from interrupting each other (no small task).

Beginning right after Friedman's report, the second half of "What's Wrong with Our Schools?" has the argumentative dynamic of a policy debate carried out as a roundtable discussion. Just as in a policy debate, the moderator, McKenzie, poses a controversial statement, or resolution, on which the participants take a position: "Market innovation is the surest way to improve the quality and promote innovation in education."[32] Instead of a series of timed speeches alternating between the sides of the controversy—as would be expected in a formal debate—the debaters, seated in a circle, discuss the topic under McKenzie's moderation. Their debate in a discussion format is not much different from the kind of policy discourse featured on political talk shows like *The MacNeil/Lehrer Report* or

Meet the Press. Unlike those two shows, though, the *Free to Choose* series had no commitment to bipartisanship guiding its format. As Friedman brings the blame narrative he developed in the first half of "What's Wrong with Our Schools?" to bear on the other debaters in the discussion, he damages their credibility. At the same time, Friedman also damages the credibility of the entire deliberation by undermining the fairness needed for it to be a meaningful competition of ideas.

"What's Wrong with Our Schools?" appears to give the question of school vouchers a fair hearing through an open discussion. Indeed, the hearing appears more than fair because Friedman and his only conditionally supportive ally, Coons, are outnumbered three to two as they take on preeminent education policy experts. However, the structure of the episode favors Friedman's position. The first half of "What's Wrong with Our Schools?" serves as Friedman's opening speech in the debate. His newsmagazine-style report on the state of the public schools not only gives him thirty minutes up front to make his case, but also the opportunity to present a framework for evaluating the subsequent debate that is favorable for his position. The overall effect of "What's Wrong with Our Schools?" is the appearance of exactly the sort of market competition between ideas that Friedman's capitalist framework prescribes for education, but carried out in a context subtly biased by blame. Friedman leverages his blame narrative from the first half of "What's Wrong with Our Schools?" to limit his opponents' rhetorical agency and turn their advantages into liabilities. He uses blame to paint the education experts as blindly ideological and cabalistic, a corrupting influence of the expertise that presumably qualified them to participate in this debate. By wielding blame in the form of *ad hominem* within a standard-looking policy discussion, Friedman's voucher proposal appears validated by the meritocracy he prescribes for the public schools, but without actually risking deliberation on equal grounds.

The debate portion of "What's Wrong with Our Schools?" begins with about four and a half minutes of discussion between Friedman's interlocutors. In order to see Friedman's rhetorical strategy unfold, let us consider the blow-by-blow: After a narrative voice invites the audience to "find out how" the education experts "react to Friedman's analysis," the debate opens with a few terse words from Shanker, a notoriously unpleasant union leader.[33] According to Shanker, US public education is "pretty good" and it would be "foolish" to "throw out something you've got" because of Friedman's "pet ideas." McKenzie then invites Coons to respond. Coons stakes out his space between the two sides in the debate, sharing his support for a voucher program so long as it is carefully calibrated to prevent a situation "with the poor in one kind of school and the rich all in another." In response to Coons, Shanker argues that market competition cannot work in a situation where the public schools have to admit all children and private schools can turn away undesirable students. According to Shanker, difficult students are a significant handicap for the public schools in the education marketplace. Shannon then reads a prepared statement making an argument similar to Shanker's and the debate turns to Anrig, who begins by expressing his agreement with Friedman that increased parental involvement would be an improvement. He then asserts a democratic purpose for education and argues that the market will subvert the public schools' core mission. Following up, McKenzie redirects Anrig, asking whether he accepts Friedman's diagnosis of the public schools. Anrig says no, and steers the debate toward some important sites of disagreement.

Providing a perceptive argument analysis, Anrig explains his rejection of Friedman's report by identifying "three straw men." Anrig argues that Friedman mischaracterizes the US public schools as more centralized than they actually are, overestimates the one-room-schoolhouse style of education that never served a large and diverse population of students, and exaggerates Hyde Park's appropriateness as a synecdoche for public schooling because of the extreme degree of poverty at Hyde Park at the time of the episode's production. After Anrig's straw-person charge, Friedman gets his first opportunity to enter the debate. Friedman's response is the critical moment in the debate where he translates his critique of public education into a debate strategy. Unlike Shanker's insulting description of Friedman's position as "pet ideas," Anrig's charges engage seriously with the details of Friedman's argument. Anrig runs the public school system to which Hyde Park belongs. He is in a position of experience and expertise to seriously discuss his objections. Moreover, especially in comparison to Shanker, Anrig states his position earnestly. At this moment in the debate Friedman could choose to engage Anrig's substantive concerns and, at least momentarily, steer the debate toward a serious policy discussion. Instead, Friedman begins his response with the blanket charge that "the one unsurprising thing about these comments is that all of the opposition to allowing the market to work comes from people who have a very strong vested interest in the present public school system."[34] From the first sentence of his first contribution, Friedman brings the blame narrative he constructed in the report to bear on the debate. Instead of responding to Anrig or any of the arguments made by the assembled experts, Friedman stakes out his position in the debate by charging Shanker, Shannon, and Anrig with bureaucracy.

This is *ad hominem* at work. Friedman calls attention to a hidden motive behind the words and the positions of his adversaries. His comment comes across as a wry observation of a conflict of interest that puts Shaker, Shannon, and Anrig at risk for hypocrisy. Their position as educational professionals makes them experts, but it also makes them interested parties in the outcome of the debate. The nationwide adoption of vouchers would presumably be damaging for them professionally. Friedman's *ad bureaucratem* implies that Shanker, Shannon, and Anrig's initial arguments should be disregarded because of their professional affiliations. Like a traditional *ad hominem* in which the character of the arguer justifies rejecting his or her argument, the professional affiliation of the arguer provides the same justification. By committing *ad hominem* through a statement that relies on the audience's experience with the entire finished episode, Friedman is able to use the fallacy to great effect, but with little risk of detection. This is blame with little risk of backfire. Simply put, Friedman chose his spot very well. Although the three education experts had been invited to represent the opposition to Friedman's voucher plan in this discussion, Friedman's blaming strategy evoked their contributions before his own only so he could group their contributions and urge his audience not to give them equal consideration. Through subtle *ad hominem*, Friedman appeared magnanimous even as he expressed a position that his audience should not countenance the rhetorical agency of his opposition.

Throughout the debate, Friedman, when given the option, chooses to argue with Shanker, making the discussion light on policy analysis and heavy on personal insult, a tactic Shanker proves just as guilty of as Friedman. As Friedman's first intervention into the debate continues past his *ad bureaucratem*, he responds to Shanker's opening statement, clarifying that his voucher proposal does not call for the dismantling of public schooling. Only after charging his interlocutors with bureaucracy and correcting the excess of Shanker's opening statement does Friedman address any of Anrig's straw-person arguments. Ignoring Anrig's charge that he harbors an idealized understanding of the one-room schoolhouse, Friedman reasserts his claim that centralization is the core problem for US public schools. He then defends his use of Hyde Park as representative of the problems of public schooling by introducing sagging SAT scores and "widespread dissatisfaction" among parents as evidence for his bleak diagnosis. Wisely, Friedman buries his weak defense behind his *ad bureaucratem* and his response to Shanker's dismissive hyperbole; Friedman's losing debate with Anrig all but disappears as he directs the audience to consider the malicious bureaucracy Shanker's insults so aptly illustrated.

Friedman extends his *ad bureaucratem* throughout the debate by classifying—as a means of response—his opponents' arguments. The best example of Friedman's strategy occurs midway through the debate when Shanker speaks up in defense of the quality of public education. Shanker argues that unsupportive fiscal policy makes the work of the public schools harder, distorting Friedman's appraisal of the public school system. Insisting that not enough resources are allocated to supporting at-risk students during elementary school, Shanker laments that those neglected students become more difficult and expensive to educate in later grades. Friedman responds to Shanker's argument by skillfully placing it into a preexisting category: "I have never yet known anybody defending a government program who didn't say, 'All of its evils come from the fact that it wasn't big enough.'"[35] Instead of explaining how an educational marketplace might address the needs of young at-risk students, Friedman attacks Shanker's argument as typical of "someone defending a government program." Once again, Friedman draws attention to his opponents' bureaucratic-ness. Friedman's retort saves him the trouble of discussing education for at-risk students—something Shanker probably knows a lot about—while simultaneously suggesting that Shanker's argument should be dismissed as yet another knee-jerk defense of bureaucracy from an archbureaucrat. More importantly, though, Friedman's dismissal demonstrates how blame, in the form of *ad hominem*, estranges Shanker from his words. According to Friedman, Shanker is not speaking for himself; he is speaking in the idiom of big government bureaucracy. Shanker is blinded by ideology to the origins of his own words. Friedman's response does not just undercut Shanker's argument, it undercuts Shanker's rhetorical agency. According to Friedman, Shanker has lost control of his own speech, ceding it to a consuming ideology. Shanker is thus ventriloquized.

As the debate carries on, Shanker does Friedman an argumentative favor by demeaning at-risk students. According to Shanker, at-risk students are a liability for public schools. These students with "hard-core problems" take "ninety-five percent" of the teacher's time, disadvantaging the public schools as competitive institutions in any educational marketplace.[36] Shanker's derisive remark undercuts the ethos of the education professionals as more compassionate or directly concerned with the well-being of the students. Shanker's callousness, the rhetorical style he was known for, makes Friedman's decision to group Anrig and Shannon with him as fellow bureaucrats all the wiser and more effective.

Tracing Friedman's invocations of the blame narrative from the first half of "What's Wrong with Our Schools?" through the following debate elucidates blame's capacity to simultaneously give and take agency. By blaming, Friedman attributes to bureaucrats the agency to ruin the public schools, but simultaneously denigrates their rhetorical agency to speak cogently about those same schools. Folding Shannon, Shanker, and Anrig together into one "bureaucratic" position, Friedman argues with all of them at once. Not only does Friedman's strategic grouping of Anrig and Shannon with Shanker force their position to bear the burden of Shanker's often caustic rhetoric, but the grouping proves Friedman's accusation: like bureaucrats, Anrig, Shannon, and Shanker work together as a group. The education experts become the argumentative embodiment of collective agency. As Friedman defiantly enacts his individual agency in response to the bureaucrats, their struggles in the debate confirm the ideological position underlying Friedman's theory of education: individual agency is a prerequisite for success. Friedman's individual rhetorical excellence is just another proof of the axiom.

Friedman's style of debate is distinguished by its defiance. Friedman's intransigence and tone convey the certainty of his convictions and serve as a technique for responding to his opponents' arguments. In addition to labeling Shanker's and Anrig's arguments as bureaucratic, Friedman delivers all strategic concessions in the form of blame. Strategic concessions are a common debate technique. When a debater chooses to make a strategic concession, he or she will acknowledge that his or her position shares a common presupposition or conclusion with other side of the debate. Strategic concessions can have several argumentative functions, but most often help to clear uncontroversial material out of the debate. After all, if an argument is agreeable to all, it needs no debating.[37] Anrig demonstrates strategic concession the first time he participates in the discussion. Before cautioning that Friedman's vision of schooling subverts the democratic purpose of public schools, Anrig concedes that he "very enthusiastically agrees" with "the part of the film that speaks to greater parental involvement."[38] Anrig's accession succeeds in that the discussion rarely addresses parental involvement, steering instead toward points of disagreement. In addition to directing a debate away from a subject, strategic concessions can also deflect arguments by reassessing them as consistent, instead of at odds, with the conceding debater's position. Strategic concessions can even be used to build goodwill between debaters or with an audience.

When Friedman takes the opportunity to identify common ground, he couches his observation in blame. He comes closest to making a standard strategic concession at two times during the debate, when he reminds his opponents and his audience that he is not proposing to destroy the public schools, only to make them compete in an educational marketplace. Friedman delivers the first in his initial contribution to the discussion. "We are not proposing to destroy the public school system," Friedman insists, "we are only asking that the public school system should be . . . open to competition." He then adds that, if the public school system "is really as good as you people make it out to be, it has nothing to worry about."[39] Despite Friedman's combative tone, his statement actually concedes that both he and his opponents agree that the public school system should continue to play an important role in US education. Although decades later Friedman would oppose the public schools as a whole in the *St. Croix Review*, within this discussion he consistently advocates reform.[40] Friedman defends noncentralized, parent-run public schools as worthy educational institutions and implies that vouchers would reward them. Friedman's concession could acknowledge the broad agreement he and his opponents share about what makes a good school and that both sides of the debate see a need for reforming underperforming public schools. Instead, Friedman wields his concession as the basis for blaming. He refers to the education experts in the debate as "you people" and implies that their protectiveness belies their own doubts about the health of the public school system they defend. Friedman thus impugns his opponents' resolve along with their arguments as the debate continues to orbit *ad hominem*.

Friedman's combative style of strategic concession grows even more aggressive the second time he employs it. Again responding to Anrig, Friedman chides, "We're not proposing . . . to dismantle anything. We're only saying, 'Put up or shut up.'" Clarifying those words, Friedman demands that the education experts "either show that you can produce the kind of education people are willing to go and get, or reduce your size, go out of business."[41] Friedman also delivers this concession as blame; the education experts are guilty because they resist putting public education up against private education in open competition. They are defending the perverse privilege of monopoly. By repeating his concession masked in blame, Friedman suggests that the education experts are hyperbolizing his argument because they are so concerned with the dire consequences of losing their monopoly on schooling in the United States. That the education experts treat Friedman's position as one that will destroy the US public schools is, from Friedman's perspective, a confession that they are not confident that public schools provide an education good enough to compete. Revealing the silencing consequences of his debate strategy, Friedman demands that, as long as the education experts are unwilling to open public education to market competition, they should "shut up." Friedman's position puts the education experts in an impossible position by forbidding them from speaking credibly about education until they are willing to concede the debate.

Couching them in blame, Friedman's antagonistic concessions sustain the consistent appearance that he is an isolated individual arguing with a recalcitrant group. Friedman plays the gadfly to the education experts' suffocating bureaucracy. Not only is Friedman's defiant style an appropriate strategy for resisting bureaucracy, his defiance once again reinforces the bureaucratic-ness of his interlocutors. The more entrenched Friedman becomes—the more he refuses to concede even basic common ground—the more the education experts work together to try and sway him, and the more they appear to be an oppressive cabal.

Thus, during the debate, Friedman embodies the position of the individual parent standing up for his or her individual agency in the face of bureaucratic recalcitrance. That he is set against three bureaucrats appears to be a disadvantage, but Friedman cleverly turns their unified resistance into evidence for his position. As Friedman's opposing educational professionals stick together in response to his advocacy of vouchers, their collective resistance in the debate proves them guilty of bureaucracy and all its sins. After an hour of television, Friedman's position is proven by a forum that gives him well over half of the time to present his position and then reproven by a debate designed not just to feature his argumentative skill, but to goad his seemingly advantaged opponents into acting as evidence of his position. Given the falsely constrained choice between bureaucracy and parental agency, the decision is easy for the folks at home.

THE RHETORICAL LEGACY OF *AD BUREAUCRATEM*

"What's Wrong with Our Schools?" is a seminar on the rhetorical power of blaming and that power's occasional incompatibility with open and fair deliberation. Although the discussion portion of the program has the legitimating appearance of open deliberation over vouchers, blame—especially in the form of *ad hominem*—poisons the well. Upon close inspection, Friedman's efforts do more to confirm his virtuosity as a public debater and political strategist than to demonstrate the worthiness of school vouchers as public policy. Taking pains to ensure that his arguments succeed, Friedman guarantees that his deliberation fails. However, in its failure, Friedman's voucher discussion demonstrates some of the possibilities and limitations of blame as a deliberative tactic.

For instance, blame is a powerful leveling tool that presents both possibility and danger for the integrity of a public deliberation. Using blame as *ad hominem* to impugn his opponents, Friedman was able to strip his expert interlocutors of their greatest advantage and turn it into a fatal liability. Instead of being the collective voice of authority in the debate, Friedman's opponents became ideologues incapable of trustworthy speech. Blame's capacity to rearrange agency in a deliberation can be liberating, exactly as Friedman depicts it. Blame can strip the undeserving or dangerous of their rhetorical power, rendering their arguments suspect. However, blame can be used to the same effect, whether one's opponent is a tyrant, a responsible leader, an extremist, or a freedom fighter. All that is necessary for a coherent *ad hominem* is to identify a personal attribute to which unending blame can be affixed.

Blame is also a powerful tool for revealing sites of contestation in a position one might otherwise uncritically accept, but because it critiques the person as well as the position, blame in the form of *ad hominem* risks facilitating a lazy approach to public deliberation. Reminding his audience of his opponents' investments in the continued dominance of the public schools as the principle means by which American children are educated, Friedman urged his audience to question their depictions of the status quo of the public schools. His argument was not unreasonable, and had it been stated more carefully might only have enhanced the deliberation by awakening his audience to an important detail in the discussion. However, Friedman's blame grouped Albert Shanker and Gregory Anrig together as blameworthy bureaucrats, a rhetorical move that did not bring greater nuance to the debate he created, but instead made it sloppier. Indeed, just who or what counts as a "bureaucrat" is not always easy to say. In "What's Wrong with Our Schools?" some teachers are characterized as bureaucrats while others are not, and the same goes for school principals. Blame's ability to group people and positions together and provide a shorthand for judging their quality can commit the very dangerous deliberative sin of appearing to provide clarity while actually paving over important distinctions. In other words, when blame is deployed as *ad hominem*, it risks facilitating prejudice.

Regardless of its deliberative infirmities, the antibureaucratic rhetoric Friedman raised to an argumentative art form in "What's Wrong with Our Schools?" has had many imitators in subsequent deliberations over education policy. The shadow of Friedman's appeal can be seen across the deliberation over education policy, where advocates take shots at educational bureaucrats with casual ease. For example, as George W. Bush signed the No Child Left Behind Act of 2001 (NCLB) in early 2002, he cited the fight against apathetic bureaucracy as part of his motivation for the new law.

Telling the story of a "young lady from New York," the president quoted her as confessing: "I don't ever remember taking an exam. They just kept passing me along. I ended up dropping out in the seventh grade. I basically felt nobody cared." Commenting on her experience, Bush declared that "the story of children being just shuffled through the system is one of the saddest stories of America."[42] For Bush, NCLB was to legislate caring, something the educational bureaucracy sorely lacked. The *ad hominem* attack of bureaucrats as uncaring and out of touch with the needs of students was not just alive and echoing through the deliberation over education policy, but providing justification for an epoch-defining policy. Indeed, by the time Bush signed NCLB into law, blaming bureaucrats had become so rote that much of the argument went unsaid, leaving the audience to fill in Bush's antibureaucratic enthymeme.

"What's Wrong with Our Schools?" remains a unique moment in the ongoing deliberation over education policy in the United States. Despite its influence, Friedman remains one of few advocates with the careful foresight and skill not just to engage in the blaming of bureaucrats as an absent category, but also to translate that blame narrative into a direct *ad hominem* assault by confronting his imagined enemy in a real discussion. Chapter 2 will consider an inverted version of this strategy. Instead of staging a confrontation in which another is publicly blamed, the authors of *A Nation at Risk* staged a confrontation in which they blamed themselves.

2

A Nation at Risk Blames Itself

In 1980, as Milton Friedman broadcast his public attack on the education bureaucracy in "What's Wrong with Our Schools?," former governor Ronald Reagan crisscrossed the country promising that, if he was elected president, he would abolish the Department of Education (ED). Taking office the following year, Reagan set out to keep his campaign promise by appointing a secretary of education willing to go down with the bureaucratic ship. When former US Commissioner of Education Terrel Bell agreed to take the unenviable job, the Reagan administration believed it had found its first and last education chief. In his memoir, Bell described the appointment as the political equivalent of "sitting on death row."[1] Under Bell's leadership, the ED would escape its sentence. Nevertheless, Reagan's first term as president proved extremely influential for the future of federal education policy.

During his first two years in the White House, as the rest of Reagan's cabinet considered various methods for relegating the ED to an office, Secretary Bell organized a blue-ribbon commission and tasked its members with developing a report on the state of public education in the United

States. Bell had hoped the report might focus the nation's attention on its struggling schools. In 1983, the report's bipartisan committee, the National Commission on Excellence in Education (NCEE), shocked the Reagan White House, the nation, and even the secretary himself when it returned a sensational report entitled *A Nation at Risk: The Imperative For Educational Reform*. The report took an alarmist tone, accusing the public education system of imperiling US economic security. If a "foreign power had attempted to impose on America the mediocre educational performance that exists today," the report exclaimed, "we might well have viewed it as an act of war."[2] In response to this national educational emergency, *A Nation at Risk* recommended stronger curricular standards, increased teacher pay, renewed focus on core academic subjects, and the resuscitation of a lost commitment to "excellence" in US public education. For ED, *A Nation at Risk* was a *deus ex machina*. Sparking a national outcry for strong federal leadership in education, the vituperative report put Reagan's plan to demote the department firmly out of political reach.

Unlike Milton Friedman's *Free to Choose* episode on public schooling, *A Nation at Risk* was a defense of bureaucracy, not an attack. Whereas Friedman assigned bureaucrats the responsibility for declining test scores and the deterioration of urban schools, the NCEE blamed the "American people" for failing to demand more from their public schools. Extending its military metaphor, the NCEE castigated Americans for "committing an act of unthinking, unilateral educational disarmament." The trouble with US public schools, according to *A Nation at Risk*, was not an excess of oversight, but a dearth. Speaking for the American people, the report's authors accepted the blame for this educational failure, confessing: "We have allowed this to happen to ourselves."[3] Like Friedman, the NCEE placed blame, but went one step further—the NCEE also accepted it on behalf of a negligent nation. In *A Nation at Risk*, instead of forming the basis of a contentious policy discussion, blame is a monologue that both initiates and completes its rhetorical ritual.

This is not to suggest that *A Nation at Risk* failed to spark conversation. A deluge of public responses to the report ran—and continue to run—the gamut from applauding endorsements to vehement denunciations.[4] Although there was considerable disagreement over the quality of its content, there is almost no disagreement about the scope of its influence. Assessing the discourse of education policy throughout the 1980s and 1990s, Holly McIntush credited *A Nation at Risk* with having "generated a new discourse on education reform" that "structured the debates for years to come."[5] Both conservative and liberal policy advocates adopted the language and arguments of the report as their education policy shibboleth.[6] Insistently plying *A Nation at Risk*'s blame narrative, conservative education scholar Chester Finn expressed exasperation at polls reporting Americans' high level of approval of their local public schools. Bemoaning the rise of a "no-fault culture," Finn imitated the militaristic language of the report, analogizing education policy with the Cold War throughout his book, *We Must Take Charge!*[7] From a more liberal perspective, E. D. Hirsch proposed standardizing the cultural education in US public schools, insisting that it would help Americans communicate more effectively with each other. He made his case in *Cultural Literacy*, but instead of resting it on the civic benefits of a shared culture, Hirsch—channeling *A Nation at Risk*—argued that teaching "Standard English" would be a critical advantage in the United States' economic competition with Japan.[8]

Scholars of both communication and education have offered explanations for the report's remarkable success in creating a broad and lasting consensus in education policy. Observing that *A Nation at Risk* "shifted the focus of education discourse from education as a means of social and political equalization to education as a means to economic prosperity," McIntush attributes the report's extraordinary success to agenda setting infused with war metaphors, free market ideology, and individualism.[9] Taking a literary approach, Kirsten Lanier credits *A Nation at Risk*'s "long run of influence" to its convincing performance of the American jeremiad.[10] Both McIntush and Lanier account for the lasting impact of *A Nation at Risk* by fitting the report into an existing discursive genre.[11]

Although both McIntush and Lanier are correct in their diagnoses—*A Nation at Risk* did successfully set an agenda for educational policy making and it certainly qualifies as a political jeremiad—neither directly addresses the rhetorical maneuver that made the report unique. *A Nation at Risk* contains both the accusation and the acceptance of culpability. It is not just blame, but self-directed blame. Using self-blame, *A Nation at Risk* sidesteps public deliberation, presenting a monologic form of a typically dialogic exchange. Instead of directing blame at another who then has the opportunity to accept or reject the accusation, the NCEE both blames the American people for the failures of public education and then accepts that blame on their behalf. In this way, the NCEE represents its position as the outcome of an open deliberation—over who in fact is to blame—that never actually took place. Importantly for education policy in the wake of *A Nation at Risk*, self-blame avoids the discussion of the full range of causes for educational failure. *A Nation at Risk's* deliberative elision helped shift the focus of education policy making from the pursuit of equality to the pursuit of outcomes.[12] In this way, *A Nation at Risk* recast the neoliberal focus on outcomes in education from a contentious proposal pushed by the eccentric likes of Milton Friedman to a measured recommendation certified by the expert deliberations of a blue-ribbon panel on behalf of a concerned nation.

PUBLIC BLAME AND SELF-BLAME

More often than not, blaming in public is a provocative act. "Those who believe that their face or reputation has been injured or even threatened," explains William Benoit in his work on image restoration, "feel compelled to offer explanations, defenses, justifications, rationalization, or excuses."[13] Not surprisingly, accusing someone or some group of causing some social ill is typically the first volley in what becomes a war of words. Whether an act of public blame gains the rhetorical traction it seeks, it almost never proceeds without some resistance from those who are accused, even if they are not the accuser's target audience. The unpredictable, but usually negative reaction of the accused helps make public blame a risky proposition. Not only must public blame rally a presumably skeptical primary audience, it must do so despite insulting another ancillary audience that is thereby motivated to oppose the accuser. Of course, there are many ways to cope with this difficulty, most of which involve blaming some person or group who either cannot respond to the accusation, whose response would be moot to the primary audience, or—as Friedman demonstrated—whose response reinforces the accusation. However, another way to sidestep the problem of blaming someone who might fight back is for the accuser to blame him or herself.

At first blush blaming oneself seems like a remarkably bad idea, but self-blame has some rhetorical benefits. Although self-blame commits an attack on one's own "face," it also enhances a particular kind of ethos. In *On Rhetoric*, Aristotle breaks ethos down into three parts, *arête* (virtuousness), *phronesis* (practical wisdom), and *eunoia* (goodwill).[14] A willingness to admit one's own failings in order to tell what one purports to be the truth is a means for establishing goodwill toward an audience. In this way, self-blame is what argument scholars call reluctant testimony.[15] By "reluctantly" making a public statement that appears to be against her own best interests, an advocate can enhance her perceived trustworthiness by being honest, even to her own detriment. Below, I will discuss the role of reluctant testimony in *A Nation at Risk's* persuasive success, but self-blame's other rhetorical benefit is more important in this case.

Self-blame is a powerful rhetorical maneuver because it recenters a deliberation. Whereas blame directed at another person or group of people invites a controversy over the *stasis* of fact, self-blame forecloses it. For a policy discussion, as for any discussion, *stasis* is crucial. *Stasis* theory comes originally from the writings of Hermagorous, but received perhaps its clearest ancient discussion in Cicero's *De Inventione*.[16] Very simply, the *stases* name the kinds of controversies that can arise during a public discussion. Although systemic treatments of the *stases* have varied over time, Cicero identified four kinds of controversy: the *stases* of fact (what happened), definition (how it should be classified), quality (whether it is good, bad, or otherwise), and policy (what should be done about it). According to *stasis* theory, all open questions in a dispute can be classified as one of the four kinds. The *stases* are like the bases in baseball. You can only be on one at a time and at the end of the play, you have to choose, or all of the progress you have made will get thrown out. They are sequential, but one need not spend equal time on each. Every base has its own set of rules and possibilities, and as a consequence, moving a runner from one to the next changes the complexion of the entire game.

Stasis theory is most typically taught in composition classrooms because the questions are generative for writing. Students can be brought to write simply by answering the *stasis* questions. In addition to providing a helpful writing heuristic, the *stasis* questions can be used to diagnose points of controversy in a public discussion of policy. When public discussions come down to pivotal points of disagreement, those points are classifiable as one *stasis* or another. For example, when an act of public blame triggers a debate over who is to blame, that exchange is a controversy over the *stasis* of fact. However, when blame is uncritically accepted, perhaps because the accuser has blamed herself and then naturally declined to dispute her own point, the same public discussion is free to advance to the other *stasis* questions. In this way, self-directed blame pushes public discussion toward questions of definition, quality, and ultimately the point of taking action, policy. This is a subtle, but valuable strategic advantage of self-blaming, and *A Nation at Risk* hit it out of the park.

AN OPEN LETTER ABOUT THE STASIS OF OUR SCHOOLS

Unlike the vast majority of government reports, *A Nation at Risk* actually captured the public's attention, inspiring a number of imitators.[17] Composed by a commission that included influential educators and intellectuals, the report's "powerful language . . . focused national attention on public education like no other single event since the Soviet Union's launch of Sputnik in 1957."[18] Officially, *A Nation at Risk* is the report of a panel commissioned by Secretary Bell. However, the report defies the limitations of its directive, declaring itself an "open letter to the American people."[19] Like private correspondence, *A Nation at Risk* delivers its "forthright" message with "candor," but unlike private correspondence, it includes expense reports and longish lists of statistics.[20] Preserving the narrative integrity of its stern warning, the NCEE spared the report of most references to the statistical information that led the panel to its startling conclusions. Few numbers, few studies, and few other government documents are mentioned in the report's prose. Instead, *A Nation at Risk* confines its technical details in blocked sections that become increasingly numerous as the report carries on, leaving the reader to piece together which studies and which statistics belong to which claims.

More than anything, *A Nation at Risk* is an impressive collection of sensational quotes. The report's hardest-hitting axioms are memorable, numerous, and concentrated in the first few pages.[21] *A Nation at Risk* is unabashedly exhortative. It urges reform, and not just from the government officials and education experts who make the big decisions about public education. Parents, students, teachers, school board members, union members, the media, and "all who care about America" are called upon to "reverse the current declining trend." The NCEE is stern and ambitious: "If the tasks we set forth are initiated now and our recommendations are fully realized over the next several years, we can expect reform of our Nation's schools, colleges, and universities."[22] *A Nation at Risk* envisions a thoroughly nationalist reform effort and supplies both exceptionalist and alarmist rhetoric to fuel it. "History is not kind to idlers," the NCEE warns; "the time is long past when American's [sic] destiny was assured simply by an abundance of natural resources and inexhaustible human enthusiasm." Heightening the sense of danger, the NCEE insists that "America's position in the world" is no longer "secure with only a few exceptionally well-trained men and women."[23] *A Nation at Risk* matches its urgent vision of a new educational future with an equally urgent sense of alarm about the status quo to produce a fervent call to action.

Although its message is clear, *A Nation at Risk*'s central rhetorical tactic is easy to lose in the suasory fray. The NCEE's remarkably tough talk is self-directed. The report begins with the now famous declaration: "Our Nation is at risk." Painting public education with an alarmist brush, the NCEE proceeds to describe a myriad of problems facing the United States as a result of its poor education policy. American "society and its educational institutions" have "lost sight of the basic purposes of schooling" and "the high expectations and disciplined effort needed to attain them," laments the report. The NCEE's dramatic rendition of the facts, as well as the "unimaginable" consequences of US public education between 1965 and 1983, is well remembered in public and academic discussions about *A Nation at Risk*. Yet by its second paragraph, *A Nation at Risk* initiates another line of reasoning just as alarming and just as pervasive throughout the report: "We have allowed this to happen to ourselves," the NCEE declares. Corroborating this accusation, the NCEE marshals supporting facts from the findings sections of the report. According to the NCEE, "we have . . . squandered the gains in student achievement made in the wake of the Sputnik challenge" and "dismantled essential support systems which helped make those gains possible."[24] According to the NCEE, all Americans—including, by implication, the NCEE—are blameworthy for permitting a "rising tide of mediocrity" to take hold in their public schools.

Urging the nation to "renew" its "commitment to schools and colleges of high quality," the NCEE preaches atonement through education reform.[25] Using *we* throughout the report, the NCEE simultaneously blames the American people for allowing public education to deteriorate and accepts responsibility as blameworthy members of the American public. In the idiom of a militaristic metaphor that carries throughout *A Nation at Risk*, the NCEE inveighs: "We have, in effect, been committing an act of unthinking, unilateral educational disarmament."[26] The NCEE makes this case over and over again throughout *A Nation at Risk*, firmly establishing the public's culpability for educational failure and depicting each negative educational trend it identifies as the consequence of negligent policy decisions. The report indicts the American people for their failure to provide an adequate education for their children, but, more importantly, it models the acceptance of that indictment. The NCEE characterizes "our" education policy as "unthinking," lacking in both vision and commitment. Eventually acknowledging the great advancement of including more Americans in public education over the course of the twentieth century, *A Nation at Risk* maintains that the coinciding decline in SAT scores is reason to reject the era of federal education policy initiated by President Lyndon Johnson with the signing of the Elementary and Secondary Education Act (ESEA) of 1965 on the grounds that it was too administratively permissive.

In *A Nation at Risk*, blame, which is usually a dialogic process wherein an accusation is made with the expectation of rejoinder from the blamed, is instead accompanied by acceptance. To create a rhetorical atmosphere of acceptance—instead of deliberation—around the act of self-blame, the NCEE contextualizes its willingness to speak for the blameworthy American people with quotes from experts using the same rhetorical maneuver. *A Nation at Risk* reports that education researcher Paul Hurd "concluded at the end of a thorough national survey of student achievement that within the context of the modern scientific revolution, 'We are raising a new generation of Americans that is scientifically and technologically illiterate.'" Similarly, the report notes that former director of the National Science Foundation John Slaughter "warned of 'a growing chasm between a small scientific and technological elite and a citizenry ill-informed, indeed uninformed, on issues with a science component.'"[27] Quoting the two experts, the NCEE positions itself as one voice in a growing choir of authorities acknowledging an unhappy reality. Hurd's and Slaughter's words provide precedent for the NCEE's claim that educational failure is self-inflicted. Like the NCEE, Hurd and Slaughter model both the accusation that the American people are to blame for the failures of the public schools and the acceptance of the blame for those failures. Like the reaction of an audience within a film to the fictional action they are presumed to be witnessing, Hurd's and Slaughter's participation in the report's self-blaming provides a proto-audience, inviting the report's readers to participate as well. Quotes from Hurd and Slaughter create a small but prestigious bandwagon.

By encouraging their audience to join them in accepting the blame for the problems facing US public education, the commission members simultaneously encourage the readers of *A Nation at Risk* to accept a limited conceptualization of the *stasis* of fact in the larger deliberation over education reform. "That we have compromised this commitment is . . . hardly surprising," they write, "given the multitude of often conflicting demands we have placed on our Nation's schools and colleges." Those schools are "routinely called on to provide solutions to personal, social, and political problems that the home and other institutions either will not or cannot resolve," concludes the NCEE. Poor educational performance is the "unsurprising" result of a lack of focus in education policy. The NCEE's causal connection between education policy and the national peril posed by declining achievement relies on the assertion that education policy is subject to a limited amount of institutional focus, a focus that has become too broad. The extracurricular aspirations of the American people, which include helping young people deal with "personal, social, and political problems," have outcompeted traditional academics for the focus of education policy and institutional effort, according to the report.[28]

The NCEE's conception of the *stasis* of fact characterizes education policy as failing due to a lack of focus. If this narrative of self-blame is accepted without contestation, it requires that any solution to the problem of educational failure must narrow the goals of education policy making. By both opening and closing the process of blaming without having a public deliberative exchange, the NCEE garners a sense of finality for its position without risking objection. For the NCEE, a strictly academic focus is critical for successful education policy because focus is a scarce resource. Self-blame in *A Nation at Risk* narrows the possibilities for policy action by defining education as responsive to a limited range of policies, an argument won at the *stasis* of fact, but ultimately impactful when the discussion of education reaches the *stasis* of policy.

In addition to its capacity to restrict the range of potential policy solutions, self-blame imposes limits on deliberation over education policy. Pinning the success or failure of education policy to the American people's focus, the NCEE defines education policy as dependent upon the personal commitment of all Americans. Like the members of the commission, each citizen must accept his or her culpability for the educational failures of the 1960s and 1970s.[29] The individual acceptance of blame for the nation's educational failures becomes a prerequisite for making good judgments about education policy. Contesting *A Nation at Risk* thus requires revisiting the *stasis* of definition and redefining education policy from a matter of acceptance to a matter for deliberation. Contesting *A Nation at Risk* also means suffering the accusation that one is in denial, the charge that any objecting party is simply denying his or her own role in the purported failure of education policy. By defining educational failure as self-inflicted, the NCEE not only discourages deliberation over the *stasis* of definition as established in the report, but also makes the future contestation over *A Nation at Risk* more difficult by preemptively framing any opposition as unrepentant.

Through self-blame, the NCEE defines the failure of education policy as a matter of acceptance. But, to facilitate that acceptance, the commission also qualifies the failure of US public schools as the result of negligence. According to *A Nation at Risk*, the American people have not acted to damage their education system; they have failed to act in its defense. In passive voice, the NCEE laments: "We have allowed this to happen to ourselves." Admonishing the American people for having "compromised" their "commitment" to educational achievement, the NCEE answers the *stasis* question of quality.[30] The American people are guilty of a crime of omission, not commission. They must accept their responsibility for the state of public education, but they do not have to admit to knowingly damaging their schools. In order to bring *A Nation at Risk* all the way from the *stasis* of definition to policy, negligence establishes a deficit of action as the source of educational failure.

To charge the American people with negligently handling their education policy, the NCEE argues counterfactually. The problem is not what the American people have done, but what they have not. *A Nation at Risk* describes American education policy from the 1960s and 1970s as "unthinking." "Our society and its educational institutions," reports the NCEE, "have lost sight of the basic purposes of schooling." Gone too, it notes, are the "high expectations and disciplined effort" that had typified American schooling before the ESEA.[31] Establishing a violated expectation, the NCEE recollects: "Each generation of Americans has outstripped its parents in education, in literacy, and in economic attainment. For the first time in the history of our country, the educational skills of one generation will not surpass, will not equal, will not even approach, those of their parents."[32] The NCEE's counterfactual claim that the US education policy has failed to ensure an expected degree of intergenerational progress appeals to the nationalist expectation that the United States not only be first in the world at everything it does, but also earn its preeminence through constant, accelerating growth.[33] When constantly accelerating improvement is an obligation, almost any outcome is blameworthy. Arguing counterfactually eases the burden of proving negligence for the NCEE. Instead of identifying a blameworthy action taken by the American people and proving the connection between that action and some damage done to public schooling, *A Nation at Risk* reasons backwards, arguing that since the current state of public education and the United States in world affairs is less than ideal, education policy and the American public that made that policy are de facto negligent.

For *A Nation at Risk*, negligence is not a legalistic designation. It has no threshold. Negligence of any kind warrants blame because it is an unsatisfactory approach toward the world at large, a way of doing things antithetical to the NCEE's exceptionalist narrative of achievement won through strenuous exertion. For the NCEE, negligence is not just a policy posture; it is a cultural practice that must be opposed in all of its manifestations.

"In contrast to the ideal of the Learning Society," the NCEE's vision of successful American education, "we find that for too many people education means doing the minimum work necessary for the moment, then coasting through life on what may have been learned in its first quarter." Making its own criticism of educational rhetoric, the NCEE remarks: "This should not surprise us because we tend to express our educational standards and expectations largely in terms of 'minimum requirements.'"[34] According to the NCEE, policies and individual actions can be negligent, but so can language choices. Thus, *A Nation at Risk* strongly encourages action and discourages even the discussion of inaction. In addition to tempering the failure of the American people to provide a better education policy, negligence bridges the *stases* of definition and policy. The quality of educational failure in the US public schools is that of negligence, a condition both blameworthy and remediable only through action.

By encouraging the American people to blame themselves for the failures of the public education system and explaining those failures as a lapse in previous commitment to educational excellence, the NCEE relied on a superficial narrative of education history. The massive effort to enfranchise African American children into the US public school system through desegregation, an effort at the core of federal education policy during the same period that the NCEE characterized as a period of decline, is conspicuously absent from *A Nation at Risk*. The word *desegregation* does not appear in the report. The NCEE comes closest to acknowledging the costs and benefits of desegregation when it discusses generational differences in the levels of education. "It is important," the report insists, "to recognize that the average citizen today is better educated and more knowledgeable than the average citizen of a generation ago," and the "positive impact of this fact on the well-being of our country and the lives of our people cannot be overstated." "Nevertheless," cautions the NCEE, "the average graduate of our schools and colleges today is not as well-educated as the average graduate of 25 or 35 years ago, when a much smaller proportion of our population completed high school and college. The negative impact of this fact likewise cannot be overstated." Speaking of the dismantlement of apartheid schooling in the United States in plausibly deniable terms, the NCEE stresses that failing to increase the overall quality while simultaneously increasing the overall diversity of US public schools constitutes negligence. Although it acknowledges the significance of educating more Americans, the NCEE references the process of desegregation only to stress that despite it, the American people should still consider themselves negligent. According to *A Nation at Risk*, the US public schools did not undergo a necessary, but difficult process of democratization; they lost focus on the primary function of public education, the production of scholastic excellence.

In the legitimating form of a bipartisan government report, *A Nation at Risk* redefined the primary purpose of public education from the general betterment of American citizens to the dogged pursuit of measureable outcomes.[35] The report not only promoted outcome variables like test scores as the arbiters of educational success, but it did so in the context of education's relationship to the state. Instead of serving the nation by working to "apply the promise of American life," public education, according to the NCEE, earns its keep by enhancing the nation's economic competitiveness.[36] Defining educational failure as a matter of acceptance and then performing that acceptance, *A Nation at Risk* reassigns the governmental role of public education while simultaneously shielding this reassignment from the balanced public deliberation that might have occurred had the NCEE not accepted its own act of blame. Combining acceptance of the American people's responsibility for the failures of public education with the qualification of that failure as negligence, the NCEE produced a powerful nationalist narrative. *A Nation at Risk* called for education reform by blaming the past inaction of the state. Without admitting the commission of bad policy, only the omission of good policy, the NCEE preserved and strengthened the role of the state in education as it repurposed public education for economic ends. Ultimately, *A Nation at Risk* applied a neoliberal frame to education policy by insisting upon the economization of schooling, but then envisioning that economization through an escalation of federal power. Beginning with what was a progressive *stasis* of fact, *A Nation at Risk* achieved a neoliberal *stasis* of policy.

RELUCTANT MESSENGERS

A Nation at Risk was an important moment in the shift from the era of access to the era of achievement, not because it popularized neoliberal policies like Friedman had, but because it gave them an air of impartiality and officialdom.[37] Yet the NCEE's prioritization of outcomes as the arbiter of successful education policy was realized only in part by its truncating of the *stases*. Public education's tragic fall from midcentury grace as told by a histrionic government report would be easy to dismiss as mere sensationalism were it not delivered reluctantly. Trumpeting its patriotism throughout *A Nation at Risk*, the NCEE is loath to make its dire assessment of a once-cherished American institution. Trading on the strident nationalism displayed throughout the report, the NCEE's act of self-blame garners believability from the discontinuity between its unabashedly pro-American worldview and its condemnation of America, the American people, and themselves as failed education policy makers. Admitting years of American failure, the NCEE sacrifices face in exchange for verisimilitude.

Reluctant testimony is both concurrent and corroborative with self-blame in *A Nation at Risk*. It unfolds in stages, culminating in the NCEE's act of self-blame. For testimony to appear reluctant, the advocate delivering it must first express a bias.[38] That is, the reluctant testifier will not appear reluctant to his or her audience without establishing a public sense of his or her interests. In deliberations over policy, those interests are grounded in attitudes that bias the testifier toward the policy or policies in question. Then, the testifying party must construct an extraordinary narrative that justifies the decision to make an exception from that publicly constructed bias. The narrative must rationalize deviance without impugning the integrity underlying the reluctant testifier's typical stance. At the same time, this narrative must relate a sense of loss in the advocate's decision to testify against his or her established bias. With a bias established and an extraordinary narrative conveyed, an advocate may then deliver an argument that will appear reluctant. In the context of a deliberation over policy, such testimony typically comes in the form of an argument that runs counter to the advocate's usual policy preferences. Reluctant testimony thus forfeits the consistency of an advocate's position as an indemnity for trustworthiness of his or her argument.[39] *A Nation at Risk* presented reluctant testimony by establishing the NCEE's patriotic bias, constructing an exceptional narrative of a national security threat, thus justifying deviance from that bias, and then reluctantly admitting that American public education is failing, thereby breaching the NCEE's patriotic bias. This last step was the NCEE's act of self-blame.

Although the rhetoric of self-blame in *A Nation at Risk* is easy to miss, the rhetoric of nationalism is not. In her analysis of the report, McIntush contends that the NCEE's use of war metaphors treats public education as a matter of national security. Noting passages where the NCEE likens federal education policy to "disarmament" and "an act of war," McIntush detects a bid for "urgency."[40] Recognizing *A Nation at Risk* as a broadly nationalist document performing in the tradition of the American jeremiad, Lanier interprets the report's jingoism as part of a broad appeal for the nation's soul, positioning a renewed education policy as the path to salvation.[41] For both McIntush and Lanier, *A Nation at Risk's* haughty nationalism was a rhetorical means for emphasizing the importance of education policy in determining the fortune of the American people. McIntush and Lanier are correct to note the broad appeal of patriotism and the strategic role that appeal played in stressing the importance of education policy. However, the NCEE's emphatic nationalism also served to cast *A Nation at Risk* as a reluctant call to face the facts.

As the NCEE appealed to the patriotism of its audience, the commission also established its authorial identity.[42] Preceding the body of the report itself, *A Nation at Risk* includes a letter from commission chairman David Pierpont Gardner, addressed to Secretary Bell. This letter formally presents *A Nation at Risk* to the secretary of education along with some framing of its contents and commentary on its production. In his letter to Secretary Bell, Gardner emphasizes the patriotic spirit that guided the production of *A Nation at Risk*. Thanking Bell on behalf of the commission for the "opportunity" to "have served our country as members" of the NCEE, Gardner contextualizes the concerns voiced in the commission's strongly worded report as emanating from a patriotic sense of duty.[43] Whether this self-professed sense of duty is a generic component of the letter or an expression of heartfelt national pride, *A Nation at Risk's* content is consistent with its patriotic fervor. From the subject of its title to its self-assigned audience, "the American people," *A Nation at Risk* implicates its findings in the consequences of education for the future of the country far beyond the traditional bounds of domestic social policy.[44] Instead of conceptualizing education policy as an exercise in wise stewardship constituting an end in itself, *A Nation at Risk* regards it as a means for realizing America's hegemonic potential as a world power.

Even as *A Nation at Risk* condemns the condition of public education in the United States, it endorses the exceptional character of America's role in world affairs. Public education's failures matter so much to the NCEE because they threaten the "unchallenged" status of the United States' "preeminence" in the world.[45] Although the commission warns that the "time is long past when America's destiny was assured simply by an abundance of natural resources and inexhaustible human enthusiasm, and by our relative isolation from the malignant problems of older civilizations," the writers narrate this preeminence lost as tragic, thus sanctioning its preservation.[46] As they mourn the passing of a progress narrative that required "each generation of Americans" to "outstrip its parents in education, in literacy, and in economic attainment," their lamentations uphold American exceptionalism as the central value that girds their policy advocacy.[47] In the first pages of *A Nation at Risk*, the NCEE establishes its investment in a narrative of America's place in the world that emphasizes positive aspects of US hegemony and, at the very least, elides its negative aspects.

After establishing and reiterating its endorsement of American exceptionalism, the NCEE needed its criticism of US education policy to emerge in opposition to its patriotism, but without undermining it. To accomplish this delicate rhetorical exchange, the NCEE reclassifies education from a matter of domestic policy to one of international policy. According to the NCEE, education policy is critical to the United States' economic and military security. Furthermore, in both cases, the NCEE is driven by exceptional circumstances to make its dire assessment of public education. Whereas the NCEE's patriotic approach to its work as a commission is portrayed as a thoughtful expression of its agency, its negative evaluation of the state of education policy is portrayed as an objective assessment driven by an especially unfortunate set of circumstances.

Addressing education as a matter of economic security, *A Nation at Risk* relates the commission's own interpretation of globalization during the late 1970s and early 1980s. Describing an economic circumstance that marks the end of an era in American history, the NCEE suggests that it has been driven to raise the alarm by an unprecedented decline in American competitiveness. Popular Japanese automobiles, efficient South Korean steel mills, and excellent German machine tools are the horsemen of an impending economic apocalypse. The dawn of the "information age," cautions the NCEE, makes learning an "indispensable investment required for success." In stressing the importance of a strong education system for the future of the nation, the NCEE translates education itself into an economic good. The NCEE frets that successful manufacturing in Germany, Japan, and South Korea "signify a redistribution of trained capability." Making its metaphor material, the NCEE declares that "knowledge, learning, information, and skilled intelligence" are the "new raw materials of international commerce."[48] The NCEE is thus compelled to flunk US public education, as evidenced by the nation's economic difficulties vis-à-vis Germany, Japan, and the "Four Asian Tigers."

Similarly, the NCEE's discussion of public education in terms of military security, although metaphorical, also helps to relieve the commission of responsibility for condemning the public schools. Describing US education policy as "unilateral disarmament" and its resulting failures as tantamount to "an act of war," *A Nation at Risk* uses this military metaphor to position the United States as a defending nation in a conflict.[49] As the victim of educational belligerence, the NCEE is compelled to respond as if at war. As the spokespeople of an aggrieved nation, the report's authors are not responsible for their conclusion that education policy has failed, in the same way that an attacked nation is not responsible for the violence that ensues after being attacked. Once again, the NCEE characterizes itself as facing circumstances that are exceptional and therefore require a strong, if reluctant, condemnation of the current state of the nation's education policy.

Having advertised its patriotism and then found—to its great surprise—a nation at exceptional risk, the NCEE was prepared to sacrifice some of its patriotic bravado at the altar of ethos. Although most of *A Nation at Risk* is written in the hyperbolic language of alarmism, the report reaches its evaluative apex with a rare episode of judiciousness:

> It is important, of course, to recognize that *the average citizen* today is better educated and more knowledgeable than the average citizen of a generation ago—more literate, and exposed to more mathematics, literature, and science. The positive impact of this fact on the well-being of our country and the lives of our people cannot be overstated.
>
> Nevertheless, *the average graduate* of our schools and colleges today is not as well-educated as the average graduate of 25 or 35 years ago, when a much smaller proportion of our population completed high school and college. The negative impact of this fact likewise cannot be overstated.[50]

Returning to this quote, we can see how the NCEE confesses its doubts about the state of US education by stressing the displeasure it experiences in doing so. Written in an uncharacteristically somber tone, this passage is conspicuous. Here, the NCEE reluctantly confesses its loss of faith in the excellence of American schooling, despite the public school system's successful past. The United State is not, in education, a leading hegemon worthy of universal praise. Committing the patriotic equivalent of apostasy, the NCEE not only finds fault with American education policy, it clarifies that a decline in academic success, even when coinciding with a rise in the inclusiveness of public schooling, still constitutes a failure.

Comparing more academically successful, but exclusive, education with less academically successful, but inclusive, education, the NCEE achieves the delicate balance of reluctant testimony. It garners believability by violating the audience's expectation for unshakably enthusiastic flag waving, at the same time retaining the nationalistic worldview that underlies its patriotism. That is, the NCEE's preference for educational success over inclusion is consistent with its view of world affairs and the exceptional place of the United States in them. In the same way the NCEE upholds American economic and military hegemony, it also upholds American educational hegemony. Across the board, the NCEE prefers the pursuit of excellence certified through competition. America's economic and military success is established by its world dominance vis-à-vis other nations. Likewise, the NCEE favors an education policy that measures educational success by aggregated test scores. Although it acknowledges the uncomfortable reality of a lapse in America's educational dominance, the NCEE expresses this reluctant realization as an obligation—not a violation—of its exceptionalist worldview.

The NCEE's artful, argumentative misdirection rhetorically inoculates *A Nation at Risk* from some of the standard skepticisms that accompany deliberations over policy. Appearing to speak against its interests, the effusively patriotic NCEE comes across as uncommonly trustworthy when admitting a failure of US education policy. At the same time the NCEE builds trust with its audience, it also ducks a broader conversation of the social consequences of endorsing excellence over inclusion. On its face, the NCEE's oblique recognition of the advances of desegregation appears fair-minded. However, as all serious consideration of the consequences of race and class on education policy vanish into four reassuringly hedging sentences, the NCEE's insistence that education policy must be overhauled despite its success producing a better-educated citizenry falls far short of fair. Exclaiming that the "negative impact" of a decline in the quality of education achieved by the average graduate of America's schools "cannot be overstated," the NCEE delivers an enthymematic evaluation. The NCEE never explains why this decline in excellence is more important than the coinciding gains in inclusion. Its insistence on the ineffability of the "negative impact" of a lapse in educational excellence, as enthymeme, invites its readers to provide their own hyperbolic consequence while it excuses itself from making the causal connections between educational excellence and change in society. Moreover, the NCEE's strong judgment intimates that the issue has already been considered, even deliberated, by the commission in advance of any public discourse. Thus, the deliberations of the NCEE prior to the publication of *A Nation at Risk* stand in for a broader public discussion over not the just the means, but also the ends of education policy.

The NCEE proclaims to have resolved the contest between the competing demand for high achievement and equality in achievement's favor. And, using *A Nation at Risk* as a powerful forum to address the American public, the NCEE suggests that the American people move forward, without deliberating over the purpose of education themselves.[51] All of this the NCEE achieves through reluctant testimony, rendering its aggressive—and ultimately quite successful—bid to reframe American education policy a passive reaction undertaken out of necessity.

THE RHETORICAL LEGACY OF SUCCESSFUL SELF-BLAME

In his letter submitting *A Nation at Risk* to Secretary Bell, Chairman Gardner declared the intentions of the NCEE: "Our purpose has been to help define the problems afflicting American education and to provide solutions, not to search for scapegoats."[52] Upon careful consideration, Gardner's prohibition was tremendously precise. Gardner did not proscribe blame, just the unnecessary search for where to place it. Indeed, when the blameworthy are already in the room, there is no need to search for them.

Looking back at *A Nation at Risk*, many scholars now find it a crucial moment in the emergence of contemporary education policy. Considering the report's legacy, Dana Goldstein observes that both its "rhetoric and policy" have proven remarkably "enduring" over the long run, supplying the "assumptions and ideals" that "underlie No Child Left Behind, Race to the Top, the Common Core, and almost every other contemporary reform effort to improve teaching."[53] This long run of influence is a testament to the effectiveness of self-directed blame. By making and then accepting its own accusation, the NCEE took an argumentative shortcut from the *stasis* of fact straight through to the *stasis* of policy, entrenching the pursuit of achievement as a core assumption of education policy making. According to *A Nation at Risk*, the failures of education policy required citizens to accept their own role in the decline of American educational achievement, not to deliberate them. Blame, an invitation to dialogue—however contentious—became a monologue instead. Delivered as reluctant testimony, the NCEE's act of self-blame not only sought to foreclose a site of public deliberation, it also simultaneously appealed for the public's trust. The NCEE established and then disrupted a patriotic ethos that provided a reluctant posture from which it could endorse, out of necessity, education policy's role in the economic and military security of the United States over the examination of equality's role in the making of education policy. Although Gardner lauded the NCEE's members for "reflecting" the "diversity" of views of the American public, *A Nation at Risk* did not reflect much on diversity when recommending new policy.[54] This preference for educational achievement over equity, made convincing through a sleight of blame, is the assumption underlying the contemporary reform efforts in which Goldstein sees *A Nation at Risk's* reflection. In her words, *A Nation at Risk* "set the terms of a debate we are still having today."[55]

In her work comparing the presidential rhetoric of accountability from the Reagan administration with that of the George W. Bush administration, Rebecca Kuehl concludes that, for both White Houses, accountability—an outgrowth of *A Nation at Risk*—framed education policy as an issue of political liberalism. Kuehl is correct, *A Nation at Risk* helped neoliberalize US education policy by framing it as a private matter of acceptance.[56] But in addition, the report's authors—by blaming themselves as American citizens—modeled the process by which each individual citizen could take personal responsibility for education policy, by raising his or her expectations. Returning once more to Gardner's letter to Bell, the chairman promised success "if the people of our country . . . care enough and are courageous enough to do what is required."[57] That is, if each and every one of the American people could find the courage to blame themselves for the failures of public education and to set aside their concerns about equality and inclusion, they could build an exceptional system of education befitting an exceptionalist nation.

3

Jonathan Kozol Blames East St. Louis

The influence of *A Nation at Risk* on the education policy of the 1990s and 2000s cannot be overstated. According to historian Patricia Albjerg Graham, *A Nation at Risk* shifted the focus of education policy makers from the pursuit of access to the pursuit of achievement. The report initiated what Graham calls the "Era of Achievement," a policy-making paradigm that seeks higher test scores through higher standards.[1] Affixing responsibility for educational failure to the American people themselves, *A Nation at Risk* blamed educational failure on an underachieving nation, an account that took hold of education reform in the late 1980s and continues to direct it more than thirty years later.[2] But no political position, however dominant, is without alternatives.

Beginning in the 1960s with his best-selling book *Death at an Early Age*, Jonathan Kozol has for decades provided a persuasive alternative to achievement.[3] A holdover from what Graham calls the "Era of Access," Kozol blames America's educational shortcomings on its failures to desegregate education and housing. Instead of advocating policies aimed at creating greater achievement through a focus on standards and testing, Kozol's alternative prescribes greater racial integration, prioritizing the improvement of equality over achievement. In his effort to inspire a renewed commitment to creating a more equal America, Kozol wrote a series of popular books centered around captivating accounts of racial and socioeconomic injustice. For example, in *Death at an Early Age*, Kozol recounts the terrible treatment of African American children that he witnessed as an elementary school teacher in the Boston Public Schools. Ending with his dismissal for teaching a Langston Hughes poem, *Death at an Early Age* typifies Kozol's oeuvre in its use of spellbinding literature to expose racial injustice.

In September 1991, with policy makers still working to implement the directives of *A Nation at Risk*, Kozol published his eighth book, *Savage Inequalities: Children in America's Schools*. A collection of detailed and often disturbing observations from his travels to some of America's poorest schools during the late 1980s, *Savage Inequalities* argued that the persistence and perniciousness of racial segregation was to blame for the failures of America's public schools. "What startled me the most," said Kozol, reflecting on the travel he had done to write the book, "was the remarkable degree of racial segregation that persisted everywhere."[4] To focus the nation's attention on the resegregation of public education, Kozol combined vivid descriptions of socioeconomic inequality with equally vivid descriptions of physical geography, tracing inequalities entrenched across the American landscape.

The public reception of *Savage Inequalities* was effusively positive. Kozol's reviewers almost universally cosigned his urgent call for reform. For the first time in its 119-year history, *Publishers Weekly*—the publishing industry's trade magazine of record—freely endorsed a book on its cover, forgoing some thirty thousand dollars in advertising revenue typically received for selling it as ad space.[5] In its place, *Publishers Weekly* printed an open letter to President George H. W. Bush "urging" him to read the "startling and disturbing new book."[6] Unfortunately for Kozol, the lesson most often drawn from *Savage Inequalities* was the need to equalize funding between public schools, not his call for an end to "racially segregated education."[7] In an interview with the *New York Times*, vice president of Cahners Publishing Fred Ciporen explained that the decision to run the letter on the cover of *Publishers Weekly* was made "unanimously" by the magazine's editorial staff. Accounting for their sudden outburst of editorial activism, Ciporen confessed: "We were very moved by this book."[8]

The editorial staff at *Publishers Weekly* was not alone. Even the ordinarily phlegmatic President Bush was moved to remark on Kozol's book.[9] Although he declined to respond directly to the *Publishers Weekly* cover letter, immediately following the book's publication he repeatedly addressed the poor state of many American schools. At a public event honoring the nation's Blue Ribbon Schools, Bush described "American education" as "anything but good," and grudgingly acknowledged the "necessary business" of "shining light into the dark corners of the system."[10] Taking advantage of the media's interest in federal education policy, Bush delivered an address on his Goals 2000 initiative to a group of Ohio educators in late November. Calling it "a revolution against business as usual," Bush stressed that Goals 2000 would help give "poor working people" the "power to choose" what public school their children would attend.[11] Arguing in favor of school choice as opposed to increased funding, the president joined the chorus of concern for the plight of poor children in America's schools. However, Bush advocated school choice as an efficient means to improve the quality of schooling through market competition, not as a means to achieve more thorough desegregation.

Bush's resistant reading of *Savage Inequalities* is not surprising, given Kozol's left-leaning politics and the president's role as the Republican party chief, but even *Publishers Weekly*—whose cover positioned the magazine as being for Kozol and against Bush—ignored Kozol's insistence for desegregation. Its cover letter admonished the Bush administration for advocating "market terms that have no place in a debate on the needs of our poor children." However, instead of calling for the reunion of black and white or even poor and wealthy children under one schoolhouse roof, *Publishers Weekly* concluded that "we will have to spend money, and a lot of it, to bring genuine equality to our schools."[12] Despite making a dramatic impression on an influential and sympathetic group of readers, Kozol's masterful book failed to secure the change he sought in either policy or rhetoric. Almost everyone who wrote about *Savage Inequalities* seemed to agree that it was a moving book deserving of praise and attention, but almost no one wrote in favor of its core argument. Although it was a passionate plea to desegregate the US public school system, *Savage Inequalities* was represented by both critics and supporters as a compelling case for funding reform. How could this be?

As critics weighed in on *Savage Inequalities*, they tended to ground their endorsement in the events Kozol recalled in its first chapter. Epitomizing the expressive prose that has made Kozol's work so popular, "Life on the Mississippi: East St. Louis, Illinois," likened the destitute Midwestern town to a third world city. Reviewing for *USA Today*, Robert Wilson declared that "everyone should read this book." Explaining why Kozol's book deserved the attention of every literate American, Wilson paraphrased many of Kozol's descriptions of East St. Louis. "Holes in the roof," "over- or under-heated buildings," and "trash-strewn lots" all make it into Wilson's review, giving his readers a feel for the aesthetic content of the book, even as its argument for desegregation was lost in favor of funding reform.[13] Moreover, Wilson was not alone. The *New York Times* ran two reviews of *Savage Inequalities*, both repeating Kozol's third world metaphor. Andrew Hacker expressed outrage over "decaying schools" and "third world conditions," while Herbert Mitgang sarcastically speculated that poor schools "might find a more sympathetic reception in Washington if they applied for help under some foreign aid program as an underdeveloped third world country."[14] Mitgang's sardonic recommendation envisioned the unlikely scenario in which a bid for federal education funds succeeded through the realization of Kozol's metaphor. Although

Mitgang was moved to imaginative sarcasm, he was not similarly moved to imagine desegregation as a policy solution—nor was Hacker.

In 2005, Kozol added his own voice to the other critics' with *The Shame of the Nation: The Restoration of Apartheid Schooling in America*, a follow-up in both form and content to *Savage Inequalities*. Like its predecessor, *The Shame of the Nation* is an unsettling log of Kozol's observations traveling to some of America's most disadvantaged public schools.[15] Extending his thesis from *Savage Inequalities*, Kozol again vehemently condemned the consequences of segregated education. Late in the book, reflecting on his own role in the previous forty years of education politics, Kozol lamented that he had hoped *Savage Inequalities* would inspire a "response" to "racial isolation" in American schools. Relating a conversation with *Washington Post* editorialist Roger Wilkins, Kozol rationalized the nation's failure to address educational inequality by attributing it to political intransigence.[16] Instead, I argue that Kozol's third world metaphor, however unintentionally, achieved precisely the response it envisioned. "Life on the Mississippi" depicted educational failure in East St. Louis as a third world problem, suggesting a third world solution: philanthropy. Americans do not address policy problems in the third world by desegregating it; we send money. Despite Kozol's stated preference for desegregation as a policy solution, *Savage Inequalities*' moving metaphorical descriptions of a third world America made a compelling case for funding reform, not integration.

PUBLIC BLAME AND METAPHOR

Before proceeding to a textual analysis of the metaphorical content of *Savage Inequalities*, it will help to discuss the relationship between blame and metaphor as rhetorical devices. That a Jonathan Kozol book engages in blaming should be a surprise to no one who works or studies in education. Moreover, an analysis of metaphors might at first blush sound like a junior high literature exercise. Yet, there is concern among education scholars that Kozol may not have gotten it entirely right in East St. Louis, and the substantial scholarly discussion of the often surprising persuasive functions of metaphors could help explain why.[17] As multifaceted rhetorical devices, metaphors can have unintended consequences, especially when used to place blame.

Metaphors are a way of making sense of the world and communicating that sense to others. In his essay "The Four Master Tropes," the twentieth century's most influential rhetorical theorist, Kenneth Burke, describes metaphor as "a device for seeing something *in terms of* something else. It brings out the thisness of that, or the thatness of this."[18] For Burke, a metaphor is a rhetorical device that underscores particular aspects of a subject by introducing a comparison. This process of comparison is especially useful when the object that is used to facilitate understanding is familiar to an audience, with features that bear out the comparison.

Of course, the two things compared in a metaphor are never identical. "Like a screen," rhetoric scholar Leah Ceccarelli explains, "metaphor filters and transforms our perceptions."[19] In the words of Emily Dickinson, metaphors "tell all the truth, but tell it slant."[20] Through comparison, metaphors invite us to see a person, place, or thing in a particular light, and this means deflecting certain comparisons just as much as it means inviting others. Additionally, metaphors have "entailments," dimensions of their comparisons that go unstated but bear on their persuasive efforts.[21] For example, when President George W. Bush referred to the war on terrorism as a "crusade" in a conversation with reporters on September 16, 2001, he likely meant for his metaphor to highlight how the American military response to the attacks of September 11 would "take a while," requiring zeal and persistence.[22] However, his use of the word *crusade* worried some US allies, because it entailed a war of conquest and religious strife.[23]

Though there is a long-standing scholarly discussion of metaphor, there is no such discussion of the relationship between metaphor and blame.[24] As a means for effecting blame, metaphors help broaden the possibilities for who or what can be blamed. Typically, when an advocate uses blame in public, he or she must, at some point, level an accusation in clear terms against a particular person or group. Even in a case of self-blame like that in *A Nation at Risk*, the National Commission on Excellence in Education was clear that responsibility for educational failure lay with the whole of the American people. However, when an accusation is made through metaphor, objects or concepts that do not normally have agency at all, let alone the agency to act otherwise and therefore be candidates for blame are granted such agency through their metaphoric representation.[25] This habit of argument appears in everyday language when agency is granted to an inanimate object or concept. For example, one might say that a bad neighborhood has ruined a young man or that a new policy is a game-changer. Not all uses of metaphor grant agency, especially metaphors that have been literalized.[26] There is, after all, a sense in which all language is representation and therefore metaphoric. Nonetheless, some metaphors not only grant agency to previously inert places or things, but also use that agency to hold those places or things responsible for the creation or persistence of various social ills.

In *Savage Inequalities*, Kozol blamed both residual de jure and creeping de facto segregation for the rampant educational failures he witnessed in East St. Louis and other poor cities. Moreover, he dramatized his act of blame with vivid descriptions of the segregated geography he found across America, choosing in the case of East St. Louis to liken the town to a third world city. In other words, Kozol placed blame by blaming place, and his use of metaphor created a powerful call to address the problem of inequality in American education. However, it also carried entailments, including the risk that those reading the book might assume philanthropy, in the form of funding reform, was the remedy his book sought.

BLAME ON THE MISSISSIPPI

The book's first chapter, "Life on the Mississippi: East St. Louis, Illinois," is a captivating exposé of the horrendous conditions in one the United States' most impoverished cities and the similarly horrendous consequences those conditions had for schoolchildren in the late 1980s. In East St. Louis, Kozol describes the "savage" landscape of "another world" blighted by a "lagoon of sewage," a "mountain of tin cans," and "acres of smoldering garbage."[27] Using the sobriquet "America's Soweto," Kozol's chapter-long metaphor rhetorically transports East St. Louis to the distant and foreboding "third world."[28] Kozol's visit to East St. Louis forms *Savage Inequalities'* most moving chapter by far. Dense with descriptive detail, "Life on the Mississippi" is a tour de force of "words facilitating vision."[29] Narrating his literal tour of the destitute city, Kozol encourages his audience to envision a postcolonial hellscape with scene after awful scene of urban decay. Although the episodes Kozol relates are horrific enough without embellishment, his descriptions exceed blank reportage. Providing the "materials on which judgment is built," Kozol translates his experiences into third world terms.[30] He cultivates his audience's perceptions and their outrage with metaphor stressing the otherness of East St. Louis's physical geography and the dysfunction of its institutions while enumerating the human costs entailed by the city's struggle.

Quoting from an article in the *St. Louis Post-Dispatch*, Kozol informs his audience on the chapter's first page that East St. Louis is "another world."[31] As Kozol describes what he witnessed in Central Illinois, scenes of urban decline become the geographic features of a malevolent, foreign landscape. Riding down Missouri Avenue, a large hole in a vacant lot becomes a "crater." Emissions from the Pfizer and Monsanto plants "cloud" the city's skies.[32] Again and again, Kozol describes artificial phenomena in natural terms as the features of a hostile land, akin to the inhospitable equatorial locales that typified European colonialism. For example, each time Kozol confronts the confounding problems created by East St. Louis's dysfunctional sewage system, he reports his encounter with an alluvial designation. On his first trip to Villa Griffin, a government housing project, Kozol surveys an "oozing lake of tainted water." Returning to the project, Kozol's sarcasm rises with the level of the lake he rechristens a "lagoon of sewage." When Kozol walks the grounds at Villa Griffin with some of its youngest residents, he finds himself traversing a "sewage marsh" in the shadow of a "mountain of tin cans."[33] The disfigured terrain Kozol recounts at the Villa Griffin simultaneously emphasizes both the exoticness and the hostility of East St. Louis's urban geography. Using geographic terms that rarely apply to the midwestern United States, like *crater* and *lagoon*, Kozol stresses the distance and otherness of East St. Louis. For Kozol, East St. Louis's problems, educational and otherwise, arise from its third world geography.

Like a metropolitan visiting a colony, Kozol tours East St. Louis with a guide. Safir Ahmed, a reporter for the *Saint Louis Post-Dispatch*, gives Kozol the lay of the land, translating the significance of its prominent places. Kozol relates Ahmed's descriptions to certify his colonial conceit. Despite East St. Louis's location near the center of the continental United States, Ahmed explains that those closest to it most comfortably regard East St. Louis as distant. To illustrate his point, Ahmed describes the Martin Luther King Jr. Bridge, a three-minute drive connecting East St. Louis directly with downtown St. Louis via Missouri Avenue. "For White people," says Ahmed, "it could be a thousand miles long."[34] According to Kozol, East St. Louis's vertigo-inducing bridge helps St. Louis and its suburbs maintain the sense of distance from East St. Louis that confirms Kozol's third world metaphor.[35]

Kozol describes how those who live near East St. Louis are deceived by a colonial landscape that distorts perceptions, but those who live *in* East St. Louis suffer a worse fate; they themselves are distorted. East St. Louis is not just distant land; it is toxic land. From years of unchecked industrial pollution, East St. Louis's soil contains heavy metals and other poisons that "chip away" at the "potential" of its children. Arsenic, mercury, lead, and even bovine steroids putrefy the ground. Outdoor play at a city park or family home, normally healthy activities, entail dangerous consequences.

In one of *Savage Inequalities'* most disturbing passages, Kozol reports on the unusually high rate of lead poisoning among children in East St. Louis. Relating a case affecting five children in just one home, Kozol lists the "insidious" symptoms of lead poisoning: "child sleep disorders, stomach pains, and hyperactive behavior."[36] Through this dark anecdote, Kozol exhumes the origins of pediatric disorders from the city's substrate. Inequality in Kozol's East St. Louis is autochthonous; it arises from the earth itself.

Having established East St. Louis's geographic distance and hostility, Kozol connects those observations to the city's dysfunctional public institutions, especially its schools. Like in a third world country, enterprises designed to improve the public welfare end up doing harm through corruption and mismanagement. Kozol begins his inspection of the East St. Louis public school system by establishing the relationship between the city's warped geography and its struggling schools. Introducing his discussion, Kozol quips: "The problems of the streets" often "spill over into the public schools."[37] Then, rendering his metaphor literal, Kozol recounts two episodes of sewage backups flooding East St. Louis schools from the inside out. Foregrounding the exceptional horror of sewage in "food preparation areas," Kozol turns his discussion to the refusal of public officials to aid the city.[38] "Life on the Mississippi" singles out Illinois governor Jim Thompson for special condemnation due to the "dismissive" tone the governor takes toward the situation in East St. Louis. Contrasting the shocking reality of a fecal deluge with the refusal of the state's highest official to entertain interventions, Kozol brings to mind the callousness and desperation of colonial rule, again incorporating the city's schools into his third world metaphor.

As Kozol relates his conversations with teachers and students in East St. Louis, he enumerates instances of institutional mismanagement. Kozol reports everything from missing paychecks to deteriorating facilities. The auto shop teacher shares a story of debilitating institutional inefficiency, explaining that, in order to bring a car into shop class, he must first move it through two other classrooms. A science teacher named Mr. McMillan tells Kozol that he cannot wear a tie to school because the climate control system is broken in his classroom. Like a colonial officer struggling with the heat of the tropics, Mr. McMillan works through one-hundred-degree days, even in the middle of winter. Mr. Solomon, a history teacher, describes East St. Louis High as temporally "cut off." With hopelessly out-of-date audiovisual equipment and textbooks, advances in pedagogy pass the students by. Their schools lack the infrastructure, such as VCRs, to implement new curricula. Kozol's scholastic tour stresses the distance—both spatial and temporal—between the colonial East St. Louis and even its neighboring suburbs.[39]

In addition to his talks with teachers and administrators, Kozol also shares his conversations with students. In Mr. Solomon's advanced class, Kozol asks a small group of high school students for their thoughts on growing up and going to school in East St. Louis. They relate some of the unfortunate and all-too-predictable experiences of growing up poor and black in the United States. One young lady recounts her experience with a prejudiced shop owner when visiting a bookstore in an adjacent suburb. Another laments the absence of Latin from East St. Louis High's curriculum. Driving at the thesis of the book he was—at the time—planning, Kozol asks the students to state their preference between funding reform and desegregation: "If the government would put a huge amount of money into East St. Louis, so that this could be a modern, well-equipped and top-rate school . . . would you say that racial segregation was no longer of importance?" In a response Kozol characterizes as representative of the class, a student named Luther comes down definitively on the side of desegregation: "Going to a school with all the races is more important than a modern school."[40] Having presented emic testimony in favor of desegregation over funding reform in the first chapter of *Savage Inequalities*, how could the book's reviewers have misrepresented Kozol's preference as being for funding reform, and why did they do so with such remarkable consistency?

By page thirty, where Kozol begins reporting his conversation with Mr. Solomon's students, "Life on the Mississippi" has thoroughly established the grim case for the third world condition of East St. Louis. In conversation with Kozol, even the students themselves express doubt about the status of their citizenship. Referring to the chasm between the quality of education in East St. Louis and other towns in Illinois, one girl asks the rhetorical question: "Are we citizens of East St. Louis or America?"[41] When Luther finally expresses his preference to go to "a school with all the races," his comment is contextualized as a brave stand against prevailing wisdom by both Kozol and the teacher. Kozol quotes Mr. Solomon marveling that Luther and his classmates "still believe in that [Martin Luther King's] dream."[42] Although the passage invites readers to share Mr. Solomon's reverence for his students' perseverance and vision, it also suggests that their belief in the power of desegregation is—or at least is popularly perceived as—naïve. Instead of explicitly encouraging his readers to support desegregation, "Life on the Mississippi" encourages them to support the students themselves on the grounds that their faith in desegregation is an admirable stance in the face of a popular tyranny. Having positioned his readers as the privileged citizens of a wealthy metropol attending—through their reading of *Savage Inequalities*—to the problems of a neglected colony, Kozol inadvertently effaces the students' agency. When one student worries aloud about her citizenship, her concerns are not labeled naïve, but when Luther shares his prioritization of desegregation over funding reform, his rational choice to put one course of action ahead of the other is interpreted as a miraculous act of faith. Luther's policy preference, instead of constituting its own decision calculus, is incorporated—as a data point—into the policy-making calculus being carried out by Kozol's readers. Luther is not a citizen participating in a democratic process of reform; he is the colonized object of reform. Luther and his classmates are subjects ripe for philanthropy, as are the rest of the poor children in *Savage Inequalities.*[43]

ONE NATION, UNDER SEGREGATION

The geographic logic of Kozol's third world metaphor carries throughout book. *Savage Inequalities* is an extensive exercise in spatial reasoning. Kozol arranged the book's chapters geographically. Beginning with East St. Louis, *Savage Inequalities* records Kozol's observations from his time in Chicago, New York, Camden, Washington, DC, San Antonio, and, briefly, Cincinnati. Like its organization, the book's central contention—that the separation of Americans by race gives rise to injustice—is also spatial. As a result, each chapter of *Savage Inequalities* begins with detailed geographic descriptions of its location, and Kozol's landscapes are not mere exposition. In lengthy digressions, Kozol gives the reader a sense of how each place he visits is laid out with a strong focus on the socioeconomic consequences of land use and administrative policies. Sharing his socio-topographic observations before describing his experiences in the schools he visits, Kozol's geography lessons frame his accounts as injustice. When *Savage Inequalities* reports the testimony of disaffected youth or burnt-out educators, readers are prepared to contextualize that testimony as the symptoms of a larger set of structural inequalities, not individual failings.

In each location he visits, Kozol maps inequality onto the land or cityscape. In East St. Louis, bluffs "surround" the downtrodden suburb "in a semicircle," enforcing both its social and its economic isolation from neighboring towns.[44] The city, Kozol notes, "is 98 percent black."[45] Quoting a professor from nearby Knox College, Kozol asserts that the "bluffs" versus "bottoms" distinction constitutes two "tiers" to which the region's inhabitants belong by virtue of their residences' elevation. Towns on the bluffs are much wealthier and whiter than East St. Louis, which is situated below, in the Mississippi's floodplain. Importantly for Kozol's argument, the bluff-dwellers are not just physically removed from the bottom-dwellers, they are administratively detached as well. In Kozol's narrative, the physical distance between the bluffs and the bottoms helps convey the tangibility and permanence of East St. Louis's hierarchical relationship with its neighbors. Kozol's topographic description of Greater St. Louis also provides a causal explanation for East St. Louis's place as the region's socioeconomic nadir. When East St. Louis needs to raise funds for public projects or seek solutions for difficult civic problems, its municipal isolation—justified administratively by its geography—excludes the city from the sizable tax base required for civic uplift. "Although dirt and water flow downhill," Kozol quips, "money and services do not."[46] With no escape, inequality pools in the low spot that is East St. Louis, a process made visible by Kozol's vivid descriptions.

In San Antonio, Kozol repeats this high ground versus low ground geography lesson. According to O. Z. White, a professor at Trinity College and Kozol's tour guide in Texas, the "poor live by the water ditches" and "the rich live on the high ground."[47] Like in East St. Louis, the poor and the wealthy of San Antonio are estranged by their differing altitudes. Also like in East St. Louis, San Antonio's administrative borders meticulously divide the city's classes and ethnicities, excusing each from the responsibility of sharing governance and resources with the other. Supporting his contention that inequality corresponds with contour lines, Kozol follows his description of San Antonio's socioeconomic geography with an exposition of the statistical differences between public schools in the heights and their peers in the ditches. Readers learn that, in addition to higher elevations, the schools of the wealthy also enjoy higher per-pupil spending and graduation rates.[48]

Kozol's survey of San Antonio near the end of *Savage Inequalities* invites comparisons with his chapter on East St. Louis at the beginning. Not only does Kozol apply many of the same criticisms to San Antonio's cityscape that he applies to East St. Louis's floodplain, he narrates his criticism following a similar rhetorical form. Touring the city with a local, just as he did in East St. Louis, Kozol acts as an authorial conduit relating an insider's account of the power relationships embedded in San Antonio's geography. Kozol's geographic appraisal primes his audience not just to see the disturbing images that make schools and neighborhoods bad, but also to see their badness as the uniform result of structural inequality. Courting his readers' déjà vu, Kozol sustains the strong appeal to pathos he crafted with "acres of smoldering garbage" and lead-poisoned children in "Life on the Mississippi" through to the last chapter.[49] With relatively brief references to neighborhood crack houses and Hispanic children addicted to inhalants, Kozol's San Antonio chapter invokes the images of urban poverty he introduced in East St. Louis.[50] As he encourages his audience to see the geographic indicators of structural inequality repeated in San Antonio, Kozol simultaneously invites his readers to see the anecdotal indicators of debilitating urban poverty recurrent with the divisive geography that makes places like East St. Louis appear third world.

Not every place Kozol visits organizes its socioeconomic inequality around naturally occurring physical geography. In New York and Chicago, inequalities conform to artificial boundaries that divide residents, block by block, into neighborhoods and boroughs. Instead of using elevation to map inequality for his audience, Kozol emphasizes the aesthetic differences that distinguish places of privilege from places of poverty. In New York, Kozol juxtaposes the educational environment of Riverdale, in the northwest corner of the Bronx, with Jerome Park, about a mile southeast. Visiting Public School 261 on Jerome Avenue, Kozol notes its regrettable location sandwiched between an elevated train line and a mortician's office. A former skating rink, PS 261 has low ceilings, no windows, and a "90 percent black and Hispanic" enrollment.[51] Inside, PS 261 is overenrolled. Outside, it is "concealed" on a "crowded city block."[52] Visiting PS 24 in Riverdale, Kozol finds a school utterly besieged by parks. Riverdale lawns—there is grass—are "neatly trimmed" and "Tudor" rooftops preside over "tree-shaded streets." The magnolias and dogwoods are "in full blossom" on the day Kozol comes to call. In addition to "decorated" windows—there are windows—Kozol marvels at PS 24's adjoining planetarium.[53] PS 24 is "integrated in the strict sense," according to Kozol, but "there is little integration in the classrooms since the vast majority of the Hispanic and black children are assigned to 'special' classes."[54] The differences Kozol notes between the two neighborhoods are parallel and acute.

In Chicago, Kozol finds similar disparities between North Lawndale and Winnetka.[55] Contrasting the affluence of Winnetka with the poverty of North Lawndale, Kozol casts inequality in deliberative terms. Highlighting the intentionality of New York's and Chicago's engineered environments, Kozol argues that the conditions that make North Lawndale an "industrial slum" are the same conditions that provide New Trier High School's "seven gyms" and "Olympic pool." The remarkable resources and beauty in places like Riverdale and Winnetka come at the cost of deprivation in places like Jerome Park and North Lawndale. Through such stark contrasts, Kozol demonstrates that these conditions could be otherwise. Featuring PS 24's planetarium and New Trier's FCC-licensed television station, Kozol not only underscores the severity of the educational inequality he condemns, he also invites his audience to see that inequality as a choice deserving blame.[56] Planetariums and television stations are ostentatious status symbols. Juxtaposing these luxuries with poor schools in various states of disrepair, Kozol encourages his audience to see the exceptional resources in wealthy school districts as decadent affronts to social justice.

Finding grounds for judgment in the geographies of North Lawndale and Winnetka, Kozol inverts his previous hierarchy by territorializing Chicago's history along with its aesthetics. Although Winnetka bests North Lawndale in wealth, it is bested by North Lawndale in history. Whereas Winnetka's streets record a century of prosperity in undulating semicircular driveways, North Lawndale's "weed-choked" lots attest to considerable and ongoing strife. Despite the absence of any historical marker, Kozol manages to find the empty lot where Martin Luther King Jr. lived during his failed campaign for racial justice in Chicago. Reporting that the civil rights leader's former house has been razed and replaced with a "broken truck" from which pizza is sold, Kozol identifies North Lawndale as an important location in the history of the civil rights movement as he simultaneously positions Winnetka within a protracted history of wealth acquisition.[57] As with New Trier High School's student-run television station, Kozol finds frivolity in Winnetka's idyllic suburban setting by juxtaposing it with the overgrown ruins of the civil rights movement in

North Lawndale. Rendered dramatically in Kozol's captivating prose, aesthetic and historical differences between wealthy and poor neighborhoods become the bases for his readers' judgments of Chicago and New York.

Kozol courts his audience's judgment, particularly their blame, in contrasting case studies made pertinent by their common geography. The disparities between PS 261 and PS 24 are so abhorrent because the two schools are physically adjacent, but qualitatively remote. They simultaneously share so much in terms of administrative oversight—a city, a borough, a school board, and so on—and so little in terms of resources and ethnic populations. As Kozol closes *Savage Inequalities*, he turns once again to the landscape to replicate this reasoning on a national scale. Delivering his appeal for a better future with the narrative equivalent of a Thomas Kinkade painting, Kozol concludes *Savage Inequalities* by describing the panoramic view of Cincinnati from the affluent Walnut Hills High School. Recalling the style of Mark Twain, author of the original *Life on the Mississippi*, Kozol's bucolic word portrait drifts into the sublime:

> Standing here by the Ohio River, watching it drift west into the edge of the horizon, picturing it as it flows onward to the place three hundred miles from here where it will pour into the Mississippi, one is struck by the sheer beauty of this country, of its goodness and unrealized goodness, of the limitless potential that it holds to render life rewarding and the spirit clean. Surely there is enough for everyone within this country. It is a tragedy that these good things are not more widely shared. All our children ought to be allowed a stake in the enormous richness of America. Whether they were born to poor white Appalachians or to wealthy Texans, to poor black people in the Bronx or to rich people in Manhasset or Winnetka, they are all quite wonderful and innocent when they are small. We soil them needlessly.[58]

In closing, Kozol merges the attributes of schoolchildren with their geography in the transcontinental anaphora of his penultimate sentence. For

Kozol, both America's children and its land, whether Appalachia, Texas, the Bronx, Manhasset, or Winnetka, are full of "potential" and "innocence" when they are unbounded. Allowed to "drift west into the edge of the horizon," the Ohio River signifies "bounty" and "goodness." The meandering river connects Americans along its path to the Mississippi, defying the compartmentalization of land and people that Kozol condemns.

But the idyllic Ohio is not Kozol's America. The public—or at least the part of it Kozol imagines reading his book—has tarnished the "wonderful" innocence of American children by inflicting a malicious demography on them. Expressing this culpability in chthonic terms, Kozol closes with the complaint: "We soil them needlessly."[59] Blighted by concentrations of inequality, Kozol's American landscape, the soil itself, replicates its distortions in its people. Of course, soil's additional meaning, "to make foul by defecation," also attends Kozol's accusation, bringing to mind the school cafeterias he describes in East St. Louis.[60] Through a haunting flourish, Kozol renders the structural violence of de facto segregation vivid through luminous visual and spatial metaphor. Despite his inspired literary performance, however, Kozol's cartographic account of inequality failed to inspire calls for desegregation. Instead, in the shadow of his chapter on East St. Louis, *Savage Inequalities* was largely received as proof positive of the need to reform public school funding in the United States.

THE RHETORICAL LEGACY OF A MISGUIDED METAPHOR

Kozol ends the first chapter with several paragraphs despairing for the future of East St. Louis. Although his conclusion unambiguously conveys his displeasure with the status quo, it leaves his preferred course of action somewhat vague. Bewailing the city's abysmal trajectory, Kozol opines: "Now and then the possibility is raised by somebody in East St. Louis that the state may someday try to end the isolation of the city as an all-black entity. This is something, however, that no one with power in the state has ever contemplated."[61] If one takes Luther's stated preference for desegregation seriously, Kozol's pessimism at the end of "Life on the Mississippi" appears to be the author's way of expressing a longing for a better future that he believes will be very difficult to achieve. However, if one interprets Luther's response as the naïve belief of an idealistic youth, then Kozol's conclusion seems to warn against the political impracticality of desegregation as a policy option. Among those familiar with the nuances of Kozol's previous writing and activism, his preference for desegregation would presumably have shone through his gloom.[62] However, for his reviewers, Kozol's advocacy was either opaque or disregarded. In their ringing endorsements of *Savage Inequalities*, the reviewers-turned-public-advocates confused the symptom for the disease, promoting a more equal system of funding and all but forgetting Kozol's insistence that segregation is the source of inequitable public school funding.

Kozol's cynical reservations at the close of "Life on the Mississippi" obscure his policy advocacy, but so does his decision to characterize East St. Louis as a third world city throughout the chapter. His geographic metaphor, which depicts the maximum physical and qualitative distance between East St. Louis and the rest of the United States, distorts his advocacy. Through his third world metaphor, Kozol conveys the look and feel of vicious poverty so heinous it was un-American.[63] However, in removing East St. Louis from its domestic geographic context, Kozol simultaneously removes the beleaguered town from its domestic policy context.

Having encouraged his audience to think of East St. Louis as hopelessly remote, desegregation makes little practical sense. Taking Kozol's geographic metaphor seriously, one wonders if a place so distant can be integrated. Ironically, this practical objection provided one of the core reasons for the Supreme Court's landmark holding in 1974 to permit de facto segregation in *Milliken v. Bradley*. The decision—which Kozol denounces in *Savage Inequalities*—overturned the Michigan Supreme Court's order to desegregate Detroit's public schools by integrating the city's school district with suburban districts. According to the Supreme Court, cross-district desegregation would have turned Michigan "into one vast new super school district" creating "logistical problems" like "the large-scale transportation of students."[64] Setting aside Kozol's metaphorical topography, the East St. Louis he describes—however sympathetically—is not just an educational but also a literal deathtrap. Talking to a girl named Serena at the Villa Griffin, Kozol relates the disconcerting story of her sister's rape and murder. Patiently explaining to Kozol that her older sister's "face was busted" and that the "police arrested one man but they didn't find the other," Serena's story is shocking evidence of the violence and desperation of life in East St. Louis, but also a stark warning about the dangers that integrating children would face there.[65] Without any help imagining a realistic path to an integrated future, persuaded reviewers echoed Kozol's appalling observations, but replaced his advocacy of desegregation with a public policy solution more befitting the third world—philanthropy. The transfer of money, instead of bodies, promised all absolution of overcoming a pernicious political injustice, without the physical risk required to redress the underlying source of its profound perniciousness.

Of course, Kozol was not alone in his use of the third world to describe the conditions that were creating educational failure in the late 1980s. In her celebrated undergraduate thesis at Princeton, future founder of Teach for America Wendy Kopp bemoaned "the dilapidated state of our public education system."[66] Calling for the creation of a national teachers corps—a project she would successfully pursue immediately after graduating—Kopp embraced the depiction of America's public schools as struggling, third world locales in desperate need of outside assistance. However, unlike Kozol, Kopp crafted a policy solution that matched her descriptive motif. Likening what would become Teach for America to the Peace Corps, Kopp insisted that it would be "something they [elite college graduates] do merely to be of service to others—the agency will be able to create the same kind of mystique the Peace Corps is able to create with its slogan 'The Hardest Job You Will Ever Love.'"[67] Recasting teaching as volunteerism, Kopp succeeded at inviting a great deal of very harsh criticism, but she also succeeded at bringing her vision of a new educational into being. Although in many ways Kozol composed a more compelling vision of America's educational future, Kopp created a more coherent one. Her policy advocacy was a better match for the metaphor they shared, the entailments of which continue to haunt our unequal school system.

4

No Child Left Behind Blames Educators

On January 8, 2002, at Hamilton High School in John Boehner's Ohio congressional district, President George W. Bush signed the No Child Left Behind Act of 2001 (NCLB) into law. On stage with Senator Edward Kennedy in the bipartisan afterglow of the September 11 terror attacks, Bush spoke perhaps the most agreeable words of his presidency: "Today begins a new era, a new time in public education in our country. As of this hour, America's schools will be on a new path of reform and a new path of results."[1] There is no controversy. NCLB fundamentally changed education in the United States and firmly set it on a new path of accountability. Bush went on to repeat these sentiments and the ceremony twice more that day in two additional states. It was an important day for both education policy and the president.

NCLB was an important law, but not a new one. NCLB reauthorized and renamed the Elementary and Secondary Education Act of 1965 (ESEA). As a reauthorization, NCLB, like the ESEA, governed the vast majority of federal spending on public education for American schoolchildren from kindergarten through their senior year of high school. However, NCLB was not the first reauthorization or the first renaming of the ESEA. The ESEA has been regularly revised since its initial passage as part of President Johnson's Great Society legislative initiative. Originally, the ESEA was a relatively small piece of legislation, just twenty-eight pages, outlining how state departments of education and local school districts could apply for federal funding provided they could demonstrate a need for federal support and show compliance with the Civil Rights Act of 1964.[2] However, over the years the ESEA grew along with the federal government into the more than seven hundred pages that constitute NCLB.

Although NCLB was a reauthorization, its epochal reputation was still deserved. Far more than simply a much longer piece of legislation, a trend reflected in the versions of the ESEA reauthorized in the 1980s and 1990s, NCLB fundamentally changed the function and purpose of the law. The ESEA had required that states and local municipalities demonstrate a need for federal funding in order to procure it. This meant using demographic data to show that a particular district or school served a certain number of students from low-income households. As long as the school or district had a population in need, the ESEA would award the funds to help those students. With the ESEA's reauthorization as NCLB, states had to also demonstrate the successful use of the funds they were given. In the new policy parlance the law enshrined, NCLB held school districts and states "accountable" for the successes and failures of public education by demanding that they "demonstrate adequate yearly progress" in the form of "measurable" student achievement. This meant giving standardized tests to students and then demonstrating improving test scores from one year to the next. A failure to improve test scores over time could mean a number of consequences for a school or school district, from curriculum reform to a loss of federal funds, or even a takeover of the school or its district by the state.

The changes NCLB wrought in American classrooms are well documented. Education scholars have addressed increasing achievement gaps, decreasing teacher retention, the expansion of charter schooling, the narrowing of curricula, and even the declining quality of civic education, among many other concerns.[3] Additionally, the policy history that led to passage of NCLB has also been explored in much greater detail elsewhere.[4] How NCLB came to be and its ramifications for America's schoolchildren are still contested questions, but not as a result of scholarly neglect. However, the landscape of education politics created by NCLB remains relatively unexplored, perhaps in part because it is a strange place. The new law strained old political alliances. In Chicago, the city's teachers union struck in 2012 for the first time in a quarter century. NCLB catalyzed rapid reform. In Washington, DC, the school system appointed its first chancellor in 2007 and then drove her from office in 2010, but in three years she managed to dismiss 241 teachers and thirty-six principals, close twenty-three schools, and negotiate merit pay into the citywide contract. Moreover, the NCLB era coincided with the effective death of school desegregation. In 2007, the US Supreme Court ruled against the use of individualized racial classifications by Seattle's School District No. 1, designed to ensure integration. But perhaps strangest of all was NCLB's longevity. Despite its broad unpopularity, NCLB held on for nearly fourteen years to become the longest-lived reauthorization of the ESEA.

To begin to appraise the landscape of educational politics that NCLB dominated for almost a decade and a half, I again turn to public blame. In this case, public blame committed by a very powerful actor, the federal government. In this chapter I use Kenneth Burke's conceptualization of scapegoating to explore the rhetoric of the NCLB law itself. I argue that accountability, the watchword of NCLB's educational politics, was a compact and potent expression of blame holding educators—the teachers and administrators who work in the schools—responsible for the failures of public education. NCLB fundamentally changed education policy by codifying a preferred blame narrative into federal law. However, accountability's consequences have stretched beyond the material effects of the law. NCLB not only blamed educators, it scapegoated them. This is not just because NCLB held educators solely responsible for the failures of the public schools, but also because it ritualized public blaming. Through systems like Adequate Yearly Progress (AYP) and corrective action for schools that failed to meet AYP, NCLB institutionalized a process of purification. AYP and corrective action—both processes imposed by NCLB—displaced the iniquities of a troubled political process, the troubled school system it had created, and the elected officials in charge of both, down onto street-level bureaucrats who were held responsible for the failures of US education at large. These rituals of blaming were NCLB's chief contribution to education policy and they were what made it scapegoating. Moreover, this policy of scapegoating has troubling implications for the civic processes that govern and make up public education. The rhetorical expedience scapegoating offers for legislators makes accountability a resilient policy strategy, even as NCLB has become policy history.

PUBLIC BLAME AND SCAPEGOATING

Analyzing NCLB as scapegoating risks coming across as a hopelessly partisan endeavor, just another academic takedown of the unpopular law. This is in part because NCLB has already been prosecuted for nearly every educational sin imaginable by activists, academics, journalists, and politicians alike. At this point, it takes real creativity to make a fresh entry in NCLB's towering list of demerits. This is also in part because scapegoating is a very serious charge. Accusing someone of scapegoating typically dismisses the person's argument by characterizing it as vicious and unfair. Scapegoating is a popular word for the sort of blame that exchanges ethics for expedience—so much so that it has inspired an entire family of pejorative idioms about throwing: "to the wolves," "to the lions," "under the bus," and so on. Although this chapter mounts no defense of the NCLB era, it does not dwell in the interpersonal morality of scapegoating either. Scapegoating, in the sense invoked here, does not resolve the question of whether NCLB was right or wrong to hold educators solely responsible for the failures of public education. Instead, Kenneth Burke's description of the ritual of scapegoating cuts to the core of NCLB's contribution to the rhetorical history of education policy. Right or wrong, good or bad, advance or regress, NCLB was, more than anything else, a collection of legal rituals designed to tame the process of reform by institutionalizing and directing public blame.

Kenneth Burke was one of the United States' foremost literary and rhetorical theorists for much of the twentieth century. From the 1930s to the 1960s, he published eight books theorizing about the influence of art and rhetoric in the process of social change. Although Burke's interests ranged from the global perspective of world politics to the local perspective of New York's avant-garde theater scene, throughout his writing, Burke maintained a focus on how symbolic action influences those who witness it.[5] Traditionally, this is called persuasion, but Burke often invoked his own term, *identification*, a sort of flip side to persuasion. To explain the connection between rhetorical action and social change, Burke catalogued lengthy lists of rhetorical devices, many of which he theorized and then re-theorized throughout his long career. Scapegoating was among them. Burke first described it in the 1930s in *Permanence and Change*, calling it the "scapegoat mechanism." Before the decade was out, he returned to the concept in a timely essay entitled "The Rhetoric of Hitler's Battle," a review explaining the rhetorical success of *Mein Kampf*. He wrote his last re-theorization, preferring the term *scapegoating*, in one his most mature and extensive works, *A Grammar of Motives*, which is where I refer to his pithiest description.[6]

For Burke, the most important thing to understand about scapegoating was that it is a ritual of purification that, whether its participants admit it or not, always fails at its goal of achieving complete dissociation. Although Burke must have harbored some concern about the ethics of scapegoating—he did after all use it to help explain Hitler's rise to power in the hopes of preventing something similar from happening in the United States—his theoretical description of scapegoating achieved insight by addressing it somewhat dispassionately. According to Burke, scapegoating is a tripartite rhetorical procedure that, when completed in its proper order, rationalizes a set of social problems and emboldens a group of people to move beyond them. In Burke's words the ritual of scapegoating involves "(1) an original state of merger, in that the iniquities are shared by both the iniquitous and their chosen vessel; (2) a principle of division, in that the elements shared in common are being ritualistically alienated; (3) a new principle of merger, this time in the unification of those whose purified identity is defined in dialectical opposition to the sacrificial offering."[7] Addressed to the masses, scapegoating aspires to "vicarious atonement." That is, by loading society's "iniquities" onto the scapegoat and then literally or figuratively banishing it, society—usually the elites who might refer to themselves collectively as "society"—jettisons its collective anxieties and moves forward, "purified" by the process. Like animals shedding old skin, humans—what Burke called "symbol-using animals"—scapegoat to unburden themselves.[8]

For Burke, scapegoating was most analogous to a medical procedure, a cure for what ails us collectively. It is a removal, the sort of surgery that ends with the suffix *-ectomy*. As an operation undertaken at the societal level, scapegoating creates what Burke called a "dialectic." In the description of the scapegoat itself, society identifies precisely what it no longer wishes to be, the diametric opposite of the new social order it desires. In this way, the scapegoat is failure epitomized. As a social manifestation of the problem, the scapegoat gives the society purchase on something that would otherwise remain beyond its grasp. The scapegoat makes society's ills concrete, organic, and assailable. However, the scapegoat is also made up of some part of society, some person or group of people who, through the ritual, are severed from the whole. Here, I add to Burke's process a concern for what happens when society scapegoats a group of people—in this case professional educators—whom it simultaneously recognizes as integral to the purified future being sought through scapegoating.

THE RITUALISTIC BLAMING OF EDUCATORS

More than anything else, rituals distinguish NCLB from the reauthorizations of the ESEA that preceded it. The language of accountability was not new to the ESEA when it was reauthorized as NCLB in 2001; accountability began appearing in the ESEA as part of the law's statement of purpose during the 1990s.[9] The statement of purpose is a section near the beginning of a US public law that, without describing particular rules and requirements, speaks to the law's context and intent. NCLB's immediate predecessor, the Improving America's Schools Act of 1994 (IASA), urged states to take on the task of holding their schools accountable. Borrowing language from the Goals 2000 summit, a convention of governors assembled by President George H. W. Bush in 1989, the IASA called for improving educational outcomes by creating and enforcing standards. According to the law's statement of purpose, "narrowing the achievement gap" required the state programs funded by the ESEA "to become even more effective in improving schools in order to enable all children to achieve high standards."[10] This is the basic formula of accountability. Invoke the failures of public education—in this case, in the form of the "achievement gap." Then, call on the states to put pressure on their educational infrastructure—in this case schools and state educational programs—to be more effective. Although the IASA strongly endorsed education standards using the rhetoric of accountability, the law included no provisions for enforcement.[11] Without prescribing any legal ritual, the IASA blamed, but did not create a system of yearly scapegoating.

Although NCLB did not introduce accountability into the ESEA, the act did introduce the enforcement of it. NCLB was a dramatic change in education policy because it obliged the states to administer annual assessments that would distinguish between schools that were making educational progress and schools that were not. If states refused to create satisfactory processes of evaluation, NCLB empowered the Department of Education to withhold the federal education funds that had previously been distributed by the ESEA, an important source of funding for public education in every state in the union.[12] The result of NCLB was that each state created its own ritual of accountability in which at least some schools would be officially designated as educationally deficient and others as educationally adequate. By requiring states to identify and expel failing schools as a way of redeeming the entire public school system, NCLB catalyzed a massive federalist experiment in scapegoating.

NCLB stood apart from the acts of blame that preceded it because it did not place blame in the pursuit of reform, it reformed in the pursuit of blame. The entire law was a system for directing blame as a process of institutional change. In specific, NCLB ritualized scapegoating across three mutually reinforcing sections of the law. Following the original state of merger from Burke's process, NCLB's statement of purpose insisted on the learning potential of all children, dispelling any objections to this principle as not just excuses, but contributions to educational failure. In two somewhat distant sections of NCLB, the law describes its "principle of division." Through the complementary processes of the AYP evaluations and the consequences of failing to meet AYP, corrective action, NCLB "ritualistically alienated" public education's iniquities by, in various ways, eliminating failing schools. Finally, in anticipating a future where all public school students meet a basic set of standards and all public schools can therefore be upheld as successful, NCLB described "a new principle of merger" through the "unification of those whose purified identity is defined in dialectical opposition to the sacrificial offering."[13] In other words, a world where all students succeed by performing at or above the standards set forth by the AYP process. Taken together, NCLB's prescriptions aspired to replace the public politics of school reform with an annual process of institutional scapegoating.

NCLB outlined scapegoating as a legal procedure by mimicking the public address typical of federal education policy. As a result, when President Bush took the podium at Hamilton High School, his description of NCLB was surprisingly straightforward. Although he spoke in broad terms about the ideas that inspired NCLB, he did not attempt to obfuscate the accountability mechanism that was the centerpiece of his signature domestic policy. "The fundamental principle of this bill," Bush declared, "is that every child can learn."[14] According to education policy experts, such a broad assertion of the equality of both ability and rights from a Republican president denoted a remarkable shift in the politics of public education.[15] As recently as the mid-1990s, influential conservative intellectuals like Charles Murray had argued that some citizens were not in fact endowed with an equal ability to learn and that an education policy based on that assumption was doomed to failure. By speaking in such broadly egalitarian terms, Bush appeared to be endorsing a traditionally Democratic position that put a strong burden on government to take an active role in ensuring equal educational opportunity and the possibility for social mobility.

However, instead of declaring a new era in social policy making for the Republican party, President Bush was describing what Burke identified as the "original state of merger" in the process of scapegoating. After declaring that "every child can learn," the president quickly clarified his position, adding that "we expect every child to learn, and you [the educators in his audience] must show us whether or not every child is learning."[16] Although Bush did indeed assert a more egalitarian outlook than the Republican party had previously maintained, his expansive vision served simultaneously as an agreeable assertion of a popular ethical stand and a critique of the public education system in the status quo. When Bush insisted that educators must "show us whether or not every child is learning," he implied the coexistence of "the iniquitous" alongside their "chosen vessel."[17] That is, the iniquitous public education system existing in merger with failing schools, its chosen vessel, the thing onto which its iniquities will be loaded. Publicly recognizing this unacceptable state of affairs is the first step in the ritual of scapegoating. "That every child can learn" was a "fundamental principle" Bush sought to popularize, but not because the Republican party had experienced a breakthrough in how it sees social policy. Instead, Bush's Manichean conception of equality underwrote his call for accountability by recasting equality of opportunity as a clear-cut rule sensible to hold to a zero-tolerance standard. Bush sought to make the principle that all children can learn an expectation backed by the force of law, an effort that began with NCLB's statement of purpose.

NCLB's statement of purpose was a collection of twelve overlapping declarations, each announcing one of the reauthorized law's many educational aspirations.[18] The statement functioned much like the president's sentiments from his speech at the signing in that each statement envisioned a better educational future, simultaneously implying a critique of the status quo. Each of the twelve declarations was phrased so that it followed as a response to an initial overarching statement, which reads:

> The purpose of this title is to ensure that all children have a fair, equal, and significant opportunity to obtain a high-quality education and reach, at a minimum, proficiency on challenging State academic achievement standards and state academic assessments. This purpose can be accomplished by—[19]

With this first clause, NCLB described the stakes of its implementation, rescuing an educational status quo imperiled by the inability of students to achieve standards in the form of state tests. Thus, NCLB began in a rhetorically traditional position for education policy by delineating between academic success and failure. For NCLB, the difference between success and failure was determined by student performance and, just as Bush declared in Hamilton, success meant "all children" must "reach . . . proficiency." There was no room for failure.

This overarching clause also suggests that each of the twelve declarations that follow it carry the weight of educational failure and success with them as they are put into practice. As NCLB ran through the changes it aimed to enforce, it described a state of merger in which the education system as a whole contained a multitude of imperfections, but the particular imperfections also outlined what Burke described as the "chosen vessel," the figure that the law would scapegoat. Across NCLB's twelve clauses, educational professionals emerge as an important point of leverage for NCLB. Although student performance on standardized tests determines educational success and failure, NCLB was clear that responsibility for those test scores falls on educators—not students, not parents, and certainly not legislators.

For Burke, scapegoating is both a sociological phenomenon and a rhetorical process. As part of a sociological phenomenon, merger describes a beginning point in which the society and its future scapegoat coexist, fated for schism. However, as part of a rhetorical process, merger describes an exigence. It is a kinetic rhetorical situation rife with potential. NCLB's twelve declarations under the statement of purpose helped realize this potential by raising awareness about the very existence of a state merger. That is, the twelve declarations insist that something is amiss, that iniquities abound. For example, the first point under the overarching statement reads:

> (1) ensuring that high-quality academic assessments, accountability systems, teacher preparation and training, curriculum, and instructional materials are aligned with challenging State academic standards so that students, teachers, parents, and administrators can measure progress against common expectations for student academic achievement;[20]

Here, declaration one begins this process of consciousness raising. For merger to matter, society must, to some significant degree, recognize itself as suffering from some ongoing failure. NCLB cast educational failure in terms of alignment and measurement. Declaration one describes the conditions under which meaningful measurement can be taken and the public education system can know itself. It simultaneously implies that those conditions for knowing do not yet exist and that, if they did, such measurements would reveal at least some level of educational failure certifiable through comparison to "common expectations." Thus, declaration one describes a process by which society might recognize some substantial educational failure and, in fitting with both the rhetorical and sociological process of merger, recognize that educational failure as already existing inside of the current public education system.

The fourth declaration in NCLB's statement of purpose begins to bend the framing of the law back toward internal problems in the public education system by giving the law's readers a way to distinguish between educational success and failure. To do this, declaration number four names NCLB's scapegoat: "low-performing schools":

> (4) holding schools, local educational agencies, and States accountable for improving the academic achievement of all students, and identifying and turning around low-performing schools that have failed to provide a high-quality education to their students, while providing alternatives to students in such schools to enable the students to receive a high-quality education;[21]

The term *low-performing* is critical. Low-performing is a euphemism for failing test scores. That is, scores that fall below some predetermined expectation, an average or a level deemed passing. Declaration four trains the audience to recognize the iniquitous among them. Here "schools, local educational agencies, and States" are said to be "accountable" for "academic achievement," which is operationalized as a test-score metric. Thus, when students—as a population—fail to perform on tests, their schools are labeled "low-performing" along with the students. According to NCLB, having students who get low test scores is synonymous with having "failed to provide a high-quality education." What makes education "high-quality" for NCLB is its ability to impart successful test taking. The result is a pregnant state of merger in which the potential scapegoat begins to take shape. Failure is located in "schools, local educational agencies, and the States."

By declaration seven, the declaration of purpose is discussing management practices between the federal government and local educational agencies and has thereby named the merged entity that will serve as the scapegoat for educational failure:

> (7) providing greater decisionmaking authority and flexibility to schools and teachers in exchange for greater responsibility for student performance;[22]

Declaration seven proposes a trade-off: greater flexibility for teachers and schools in exchange for assuming greater responsibility for student performance. On the one hand, this trade-off nods to the American tradition of keeping school governance local. Regardless of whether the governance of American schools could be accurately described as local in 2001, the public discourse of education policy makers continued to characterize local knowledge and control as indispensable for good education policy at the federal level.[23] Presumably, under NCLB, teachers and schools were to be given a greater degree of autonomy to make their own decisions about teaching and administration. The promise is a little strange because states, not the federal government, typically exercise the most direct and potentially oppressive administrative control over local school districts and, through them, teachers and schools. Additionally, as a close examination of the corrective action process will reveal, the ritual of scapegoating that NCLB prescribed resulted in exactly the opposite when schools failed. Coping with NCLB's corrective measures became one of the most visible federal reforms in terms of the day-to-day practices of public education, requiring many teachers to, for example, write learning objectives on the board every day or begin each class with a practice exam question. However, on its surface, declaration seven seems to make sense: teachers and schools gain both freedom and accountability, presumably in proportionate amounts. Moreover, US presidents often cite the importance of local input at precisely the same moments when they impose greater federal control, and education policy has a long history of this specific rhetorical maneuver.[24]

Through declaration seven's agreeable reasoning and gentle performance of the education policy truism that locals know best, it is easy to miss that the clause identifies schools and teachers as the target of NCLB's enforcement mechanisms. However, the trade-off of flexibility for responsibility does not just reveal that teachers and schools will be the target of federal enforcement, it also characterizes the targeting of schools and teachers as both mutually beneficial and mutually agreed upon. In this way, declaration seven reads like a terms-of-service agreement. There is a contractual ring to it, as if teachers and schools have the choice and are voluntarily entering into this agreement with the federal government. By receiving "greater decisionmaking authority and flexibility," teachers and schools also accept the federal government's decision to treat them as largely responsible for student performance on state assessments. Teachers and schools are thereby made into the chief policy lever for NCLB, the point of pressure the law will use in pursuit of its legislatively ordained goals. When students fail tests, teachers and schools will be held responsible for those failures.

This trade-off was essential to NCLB's effort to manufacture educational change through blame because, as British philosopher P. F. Strawson explains, blame presupposes agency and choice.[25] For NCLB to hold teachers and schools responsible as the only point of pressure for instituting educational change, the law needed to give teachers and schools enough power to not just plausibly, but probably make the crucial difference between educational success and failure. Without the devolution—at least in legal print—of the requisite freedom of action, the law and the lawmakers might themselves be perceived as those most plausibly responsible for educational success and failure instead of schools and teachers. By awarding autonomy to teachers and schools, declaration seven reads, on its surface, as an attempt to legislate the best interests of teachers and schools. Thus, by declaration seven, NCLB's statement of purpose describes a state of merger in which education professionals are the best candidates for scapegoating, not just because they are the most plausibly responsible for educational success and failure, but also because—as the recipients of newfound authority and flexibility—they are presumably willing.

Altogether, NCLB's statement of purpose with its twelve subordinate clauses strategically describes a landscape of merger, a situation rife with rhetorical potential. This landscape has several critical features that facilitate specific acts of scapegoating and prohibit others. Merger in NCLB was a state in which all children *can* learn, but not all children *are* learning. Learning meant performing adequately on tests and when students failed to perform in large enough numbers in localized areas, their schools and teachers were considered ultimately responsible. These educators were therefore the merged entity that was an ideal target for scapegoating. Importantly, questions about the actions of policy makers that deprive schools of support or create community conditions that might also contribute to educational failure in the form of test scores (among other indicators) were not included as part of the milieu of merger in the law's statement of purpose. Despite their participation in the political process that created education policy, parents, legislators, and test makers were not candidates for scapegoating. As NCLB described the process of yearly scapegoating it would use to reform American education, this landscape of fair-minded legislators dealing justly with blameworthy teachers and schools blossomed into the legal nuts and bolts of accountability, the rituals that would make NCLB such a controversial policy became clear.

NCLB turned the pregnant merger described in its statement of purpose into division by creating a new ritual of educational administration: Adequate Yearly Progress (AYP). AYP was the system of annual assessments NCLB required all states to institute in order to seek Title I funding. In some states AYP necessitated a new process of yearly standardized testing, but in most it connected existing testing practices with new administrative consequences. In addition to distinguishing between adequate and inadequate educational achievement among students, AYP used students' standardized test scores to distinguish between adequate and inadequate educational achievement among schools. By separating successful and failing schools, AYP created "a principle of division" that loaded the "iniquities" of the public education system onto educators and institutions with low average test scores.[26] Often referred to as a "testing regime," AYP spurred the creation of holiday-like weeks during the school year where instruction stopped and the school was given over to the testing process. At some schools this even involved a bizarre form of reverse decorating whereby posters that might help students answer test questions, like times tables, the light spectrum, or how to build a character map, were covered by white butcher paper to secure the validity of the testing process.

Through these processes of collective evaluation, AYP ritualistically identified and then alienated educational professionals at schools with low-achieving students, thereby casting out the iniquity of low test scores from public education.[27]

The basic function of NCLB was the relationship between AYP, the process by which the law managed its principle of division, and corrective action, the process by which NCLB created a new, purified system. In subsection 1111.b.2.C, a subpart of "Accountability," NCLB defined AYP in such a way that it could be put to use in each of the states. Under the threat of losing access to the federal funds that had been provided by the ESEA since its creation in 1965, NCLB required each of the states to define and determine AYP for all of its schools.[28] Across seven subpoints in 1111.b.2.C, NCLB described acceptable forms of AYP: It must be a "measure" based "primarily on academic assessments" that is "statistically valid and reliable."[29] AYP may include other indicators such as graduation rates so long as it "applies the same high standard of academic achievement" to all schools in the state.[30] AYP must also identify student populations of interest, such as students belonging to specific racial and economic categories, and provide a way to disaggregate the test results that apply to those groups.[31] In order to fulfill NCLB's expectations for AYP, the law required each state to submit a plan describing how it would assess AYP in its schools, demonstrating that the state's method for distinguishing between success and failure matched NCLB's vision. In other words, NCLB required each state to create and submit its own ritual of division for federal approval.

The requirements for each state's ritual of division set forth in NCLB served a dual purpose. On the one hand, the rules helped NCLB, as public policy, enforce some degree of uniformity in the implementation of the new law without violating the expectation that education policy would remain, to some significant degree, a matter of local policy controlled by states and districts. On the other hand, NCLB's longish description of expectations for what the "State Plans" would look like and what form of

AYP they would require served as a defense of the legitimacy of the new law. To be an approved ritual of division, each state's evaluation of AYP had to be comprehensive, quantitative, and ambitious. To be comprehensive, AYP had to be an evaluation that would be applied to all schools in the state. To give the process a sense of fairness, each school had to be a possible target for scapegoating. Additionally, in order to be quantitative, AYP had to be a "statistically valid and reliable" academic assessment based on "separate measurable annual objectives."[32] Although NCLB did not explicitly require that states administer standardized tests to determine whether schools met AYP, it certainly assumed they would in order to meet the law's requirements for statistical validity in the AYP process.[33] In order to be ambitious, AYP had to hold schools to "high standards" of achievement. However, the law did not give examples of what constitutes high achievement, but it did use the terms "achievement" and "test scores" interchangeably, implying that the best practical meaning of "high standards" was the expectation for high test scores.

Although NCLB went to great pains to characterize AYP as a fair and defensible process, the law did tilt the playing field in favor of certain outcomes. For example, point 1111.b.2.C.v describes "separate measurable annual objectives" as potentially a part of determining AYP. These separate objectives could be any way to evaluate a school: dropout rates, college placement rates, surveys of student and/or parent satisfaction, etc. Presumably, this subpoint would allow a state to consider evaluative criteria in addition to test scores when determining whether AYP was met. However, in a section entitled "Requirements for Other Indicators," NCLB clarified that the results of these non–test score evaluation criteria could only be used to fail a school, not to help it pass AYP.[34] Like in declaration seven from NCLB's statement of purpose, the law implied that states and educators retained more control than they actually did. The bottom line for NCLB was that schools that could not produce high enough test scores among their students were to be labeled failing regardless of the opinion of the state or local authorities. Test scores were NCLB's principle of division.

Additionally, the law took some risk with its original narrative of merger as it described division. Recall that in its statement of purpose, NCLB insisted that its primary objective must be to ensure that no child is left behind. The implication of this insistence was that when a child was left behind, division should appear between successful and failing schools. By using statistical analysis to determine AYP, NCLB created a tension between its insistence that public education should uphold the inherent value of individual students and its requirement that the AYP ritual determine success and failure on a schoolwide basis. When NCLB clarified that AYP "shall not be required in a case in which the number of students in a category is insufficient to yield statistically reliable information," it sanctioned a process that denied some children the protection of federal oversight.[35] That is, NCLB specifically excused schools from concerning themselves with the academic achievement of students from groups too small to provide a statistically useful set of test scores. These students were not protected precisely because they were too singular to be rendered by the law's principle of division. Indeed, it would have been more accurate for the statement of purpose to declare: "No statistically significant groups of children left behind." Here, NCLB's process for realizing division was in tension with its description of an education system in a state of merger ripe for division. This was a flaw in the reasoning of the law, but not necessarily hypocrisy. NCLB reimagined the public education system through the process of scapegoating. Enforcing accountability was a new process for school reform, but did not resolve the system's contradictions.

"CORRECTING" SCHOOLS

When a school failed to meet AYP test score targets for two years running, NCLB required that state and local educational administrators intervene. NCLB provided the regulatory expectations for those interventions as well as the final step in the law's scapegoating process through a mechanism called "corrective actions." After describing an original state of merger rife with the possibility of division in its statement of purpose and then prescribing the process for prying open that division with AYP, NCLB laid the foundation for a "a new principle of merger" with two sections of corrective actions. According to Burke, the scapegoating process is completed by "the unification of those whose purified identity is defined in dialectical opposition to the sacrificial offering."[36] For NCLB, schools that had student populations with low aggregated test scores were the sacrificial offering and, by instituting corrective actions, the public education system defined itself as dialectically opposed to those schools. Indeed, the very purpose of the Department of Education as the national embodiment of the public schools post-NCLB was the effort to ensure that public education would not become those failing schools. Corrective action provided a tangible policy procedure making the dialectical opposition to low test score material, even as the policy options most likely to lead to the realization of higher test scores were eschewed.

NCLB described corrective action twice, both times as a menu of actions available for an administrative authority to choose from in response to a school's repeated failure to make AYP. For the reader's convenience, both subsections are reproduced side by side in table 4.1. Subsection 1116.b.7.C, "Role of the Local Educational Agency," was addressed to local administrators and included four subpoints, all of which had to be enacted. Under subpoint iv, NCLB provided a menu of six actions, from which the local educational authority—almost always the school district—was required to choose at least one. Section 1116.c.10.C, labeled "Certain Corrective Actions Required," included seven subpoints enumerating the actions available to the state at the same point. Like subsection iv from the local-directed corrective actions section, section 1116.c.10.C required that the state authority—typically the state's department of education—enact at least one of the actions on the menu. Presumably, in cases where corrective action was required, the state's choice of corrective action could override that of the local educational agency.

The corrective actions prescribed by NCLB were presented as a set of policy strategies for addressing chronically low test scores at public schools

Table 4.1 *Corrective actions comparison*

§ 1116.b.7.C – Local menu	**§ 1116.c.10.C – State menu**
"(C) ROLE OF LOCAL EDUCATIONAL AGENCY.—In the case of any school served by a local educational agency under this part that fails to make adequate yearly progress, as defined by the State under section 1111(b)(2), by the end of the second full school year after the identification under paragraph (1), the local educational agency shall— "(i) continue to provide all students enrolled in the school with the option to transfer to another public school served by the local educational agency, in accordance with paragraph (1)(E) and (F); "(ii) continue to provide technical assistance consistent with paragraph (4) while instituting any corrective action under clause (iv); "(iii) continue to make supplemental educational services available, in accordance with subsection (e), to children who remain in the school; and "(iv) identify the school for corrective action and take at least one of the following corrective actions: "(I) Replace the school staff who are relevant to the failure to make adequate yearly progress. "(II) Institute and fully implement a new curriculum, including providing appropriate professional development for all relevant staff, that is based on scientifically based research and offers substantial promise of improving educational achievement for low-achieving students and enabling the school to make adequate yearly progress. "(III) Significantly decrease management authority at the school level. "(IV) Appoint an outside expert to advise the school on its progress toward making adequate yearly progress, based on its school plan under paragraph (3). "(V) Extend the school year or school day for the school. "(VI) Restructure the internal organizational structure of the school.	"(C) CERTAIN CORRECTIVE ACTIONS REQUIRED.—In the case of a local educational agency identified for corrective action, the State educational agency shall take at least one of the following corrective actions: "(i) Deferring programmatic funds or reducing administrative funds. "(ii) Instituting and fully implementing a new curriculum that is based on State and local academic content and achievement standards, including providing appropriate professional development based on scientifically based research for all relevant staff, that offers substantial promise of improving educational achievement for low-achieving students. "(iii) Replacing the local educational agency personnel who are relevant to the failure to make adequate yearly progress. "(iv) Removing particular schools from the jurisdiction of the local educational agency and establishing alternative arrangements for public governance and supervision of such schools. "(v) Appointing, through the State educational agency, a receiver or trustee to administer the affairs of the local educational agency in place of the superintendent and school board. "(vi) Abolishing or restructuring the local educational agency. "(vii) Authorizing students to transfer from a school operated by the local educational agency to a higher-performing public school operated by another local educational agency in accordance with subsections (b)(1)(E) and (F), and providing to such students transportation (or the costs of transportation) to such schools consistent with subsection (b)(9), in conjunction with carrying out not less than one additional action described under this subparagraph.

that failed to meet AYP. However, even a cursory read reveals that the list of policy actions available to both local educational agencies and the state were not all designed to fix the problem of low test scores at failing schools. Of the seven options for corrective action available to the states (see table 4.1, right-hand column), only the second option—adopting a stricter version of the state's curriculum—did not represent an existential threat to the low-achieving school. Option i required reducing funding. In a bureaucracy, the reduction of funding often shrinks budgetary space in subsequent years, ultimately threatening the existence of the item or program losing funding. Additionally, there was little hope that reduced funding would increase the successful educational output of any school. So, option i was more likely to operate as a punishment for the problem of low test scores than a solution to it. Options iii through v all amounted to roughly the same thing, firing and replacing some of the teachers and administrators at the failing school. At its most extreme, option iv made it possible to gut the school both administratively and structurally and re-form it as a charter. The existential threat in option vi needs no interpretation; it empowered the state to terminate the district. Option vii involved sending some of the offending school's students to different districts and was required of the district anyway under 1116.b.7.C.i (see the left-hand column of table 4.1). Like option i, it did not threaten the immediate abolition of the school, but carried to its end, option vii would have. Additionally, since state funds in many states were determined in part or in full by enrollment, option vii carried the same bureaucratic threat to the school's existence as option one, death by defunding. The only option open to the state that might have improved the situation of a school selected through corrective action was option ii: to reform the school's curriculum so that it more directly reflected the federally mandated state curriculum. Indeed, this was the option selected so often that many parents (and Diane Ravitch, as we will see in the next chapter) complained about test preparation overwhelming the curriculum.

The corrective actions for local authorities are listed under subpoint iv in the left-hand column of table 4.1. Like the state's potential corrective actions, the school district's were mostly punitive. Also like the state, the option most likely to help the school improves its test score average was option II—to more fully implement the state's new, testing-centered curriculum. Option V, not available at the state level, suggested lengthening the school day or school year. This certainly could have improved student test scores, but it presented a set of logistical obstacles that option II did not entail. Presumably, it would have required paying everyone who worked at the school for their additional work as well as rescheduling many of the school's activities, and parents would have had to consent on some level to any dramatic change to the schedule of their children's schooling. So, for both the state and the school districts, curricular reform was the easiest option and the one most likely to address the problem of low test scores.

Although corrective action was presented as the policy solution to the problem of chronically low test scores, that impression was misleading. If that were the case, the majority of options for state corrective action would presumably connect more directly with improving test scores. Corrective action could be understood instead as a rhetorical strategy by reconsidering the definition of *corrective.* NCLB could have meant to use the term *corrective* in the sense of "corrective training," which the *Oxford English Dictionary* defines as a process of "setting right what is erroneous or faulty." This would have indicated an intention to repair the school's ability to educate its students in a way that would result in greater achievement on standardized tests. However, NCLB's use of the word might also have intended the sense of "corrective justice," which the *Oxford English Dictionary* differentiates from other forms of justice for being especially "castigatory" or "punitive."[37] This definition would suggest that the subsections describing corrective action were designed to offer ways of reprimanding school districts for failing to meet the standards set for them. All of the options offered in the section could be accounted for by one definition or the other, which could present a serious interpretive problem for the enforcement of the law. Was the spirit of NCLB to punish or repair schools that failed to make AYP?

There certainly was support for reading "corrective" as meaning punitive across the text of the law. In an earlier portion of the "State Review and Local Educational Agency Improvement" subsection entitled "Rewards," NCLB stated: "In the case of a local educational agency that, for 2 consecutive years, has exceeded adequate yearly progress as defined in the State plan under section 1111(b)(2), the State may make rewards of the kinds described under section 1117 to the agency."[38] This subsection, since it prescribed action for the opposite case of subsection 1116.c.10.C, where a school has failed to make AYP, defined "corrective" action by naming its antonym. If success should be met with "reward"—although this was not required by NCLB—then failure must be met with punishment. Indeed, the specific rewards described in the "State Recognition" subsection of section 1117 were direct opposites of some items on the corrective actions menus.[39] NCLB authorized states to reward succeeding schools by giving them additional funding and special status as "Distinguished Schools," and awarding pay bonuses to outstanding teachers at those schools.

Understanding corrective action as the final stage of scapegoating reveals a rhetorical purpose for NCLB's corrective action sections. Corrective action was not about achieving a particular policy outcome; it was about the public act of *opposing* a particular policy outcome. The corrective actions chosen by school districts and states were not terribly likely to turn many schools around. In fact, a common result of a school being slated for corrective action was that the public school system relinquished control to a private concern that reformed it as a charter. However, punishing schools that failed to make AYP did clearly communicate the public education system's "dialectical opposition" to low test scores. Under point II in table 4.1, where NCLB gave school districts the option to address a school's repeated failure to meet AYP by reforming the school's curriculum, it also clarified that the purpose of this action was to "[enable] the school to make adequate yearly progress." Thus the district was charged with improving test outcomes at the school. Comparing 1116.b.7.C.iv.II to its counterpart on the state menu of corrective actions, 1116.c.10.C.ii, we see that the language of the two was identical except that this last phrase mandating a concern with improvement was left out. The states were not charged with improving their schools. Their job began and ended with ensuring that the accountability process was completed, that the failure to meet AYP resulted in corrective action. Above all else, NCLB required the public display of disapproval of low test scores.

In NCLB's corrective action sections, the "unification" of the public schools emerged as an imagined organization made up of those "whose purified identity is defined in dialectical opposition to the sacrificial offering"—that is, schools with students who, on average, scored below acceptable levels on standardized tests.[40] NCLB's crystal-clear condemnation of low test scores provided the grounds for the purification of the system. Whatever the policy outcome of NCLB, the rhetorical outcome was an era of education policy defined by its commitment to accountability. The public school system's job was to censure low test scores, not to improve them. Collectively, in this "new merger," the public education system was reconstructed as an organization intolerant of schools and educators whose students fail to earn high enough test scores. Responsibility for making the public schools better was pushed away from the legislature and down onto street-level bureaucrats. Regardless of whether schools that failed to meet AYP were successfully reformed, the self-concept of the public school system was, and dramatically so.

THE RHETORICAL LEGACY OF EDUCATIONAL SCAPEGOATING

For Burke, scapegoating is a process of "vicarious atonement."[41] Prosecuted to its completion, scapegoating promises a collective rebirth. Groups that scapegoat emerge renewed, perhaps smaller given that some members were expelled, but also strengthened by a fresh sense of identity, purpose, and possibility. Burke's description of the rhetorical process of scapegoating helps shed light on NCLB's strategic use of language to create an education policy process that exuded accountability and abhorred low test scores. However, NCLB was not just an individual act of scapegoating; it was a scapegoating policy. That is, NCLB tried to tame the swirl of blaming in the discourse of education policy by mandating an official practice of public blaming. By requiring that states create processes of scapegoating and then repeat them on a yearly basis to the satisfaction of the federal government, the law made blaming by scapegoating the primary civic ritual of public education in the United States.

By locking the public discussion of education policy in orbit around this annual scapegoating ritual, NCLB reconfigured the process by which the American public oversees its schools. Instead of holding legislators accountable for the successes and failures of public education, NCLB encouraged parents and citizens to exercise their civic duty by monitoring the street-level bureaucrats in their local schools. To ensure that the blaming NCLB required would be adequately public, the law mandated a report card system through which the states had to inform parents about the status of their schools vis-à-vis AYP. According to subsection 1111.h.1, entitled "Annual State Report Card," the reports were meant to keep parents informed about the yearly fortunes of their local public schools. Subsection 1111.h.1.C listed eight requirements for the content and distribution of the reports, including information such as average state AYP results, district graduation rates, a view of the district in terms of its success at making AYP, and the qualifications of teachers in the state.[42] Section 1111.h.6 also clarified that parents had to be informed that they were entitled to request a report on the qualifications of any teacher working at their local school. This annual report card system invited parents to participate in the new process of overseeing educators. It also implied that educators and schools were likely to need parents to hold them accountable for the quality of their work in order to do a good job. At the same time that the report card system directed and enabled parental oversight of teachers, schools, and districts, it pushed the issue of academic achievement down to the realm of local politics and out of the national civic conversation. The legislators who passed NCLB received no report card and were not candidates for oversight, even as they made consequential decisions about things like the size and availability of education funding.

By creating a public school system defined by its commitment to scapegoating educators and inviting parents to participate in the process of monitoring schools and educators, NCLB not only reconfigured federal education policy, it also reconfigured the deliberative process by which education policy is made and remade. Instead of having citizens address their concerns and desires to policy makers and then hold those people accountable for their wishes through elections, NCLB created a deliberative process whereby policy makers and parents would issue demands to educators and then hold those educators accountable through a system of professional reward and punishment. It is not terribly surprising, then, that many educators have found the politics of education since the passage of NCLB punitive and alienating.[43] Presumably, teachers, administrators, and other educational professionals should be the leaders in forging a better educational future. However, under NCLB, educators were understood to be the greatest barrier, blocking the way to a future of greater academic achievement. The use of scapegoating by parents and legislators to continuously place demands upon the educational professionals who run the pubic schools is the politics of accountability, but it is a strange politics. By making plenty of space for parents to hold educators accountable, but none for citizens to hold legislators accountable, NCLB sowed the seeds of its own undoing.

5

Diane Ravitch Blames No Child Left Behind

By 2010, No Child Left Behind (NCLB) had become education policy zombified. Disowned by both major political parties and long overdue for reauthorization, the law threatened to terrorize America's schools. NCLB conditioned federal funding on the requirement that all public schools be at 100 percent proficiency by 2014, but despite a broad consensus that this proviso would not be met, no federal action loomed on the horizon. Both living and dead, NCLB persisted in governmental limbo, caught between an executive branch that lacked the will to enforce it and a "do nothing" legislative branch that lacked the will to replace it.[1] Although deeply unpopular, NCLB had endured longer than any other instantiation of the Elementary and Secondary Education Act (ESEA) since the original passage of that law in 1965. Presiding—at least in name—over the federal effort to improve public education, NCLB had become the principal target of the public blame game it was designed to supervise.

It is easy to forget, but NCLB was not always an unpopular law. At the time of its passage, NCLB was hailed as a triumph of bipartisan lawmaking, one of the first big legislative accomplishments of President George W. Bush, who had run in part on the success of his similar education policy as governor of Texas.[2] However, shortly after its passage, the bipartisan good feeling surrounding NCLB—buoyed in part by the national response to the terror attacks of September 11, 2001—began to fade. NCLB's precipitous slide from popularity was hastened along by a series of condemnations from public figures who initially supported it. For example, when the Bush White House failed to back NCLB with increased appropriations in the early 2000s, US senator and NCLB cosponsor Edward Kennedy bitterly denounced the law.[3] Along with Kennedy, NCLB earned a great number of liberal critics during the 2000s. However, as gains in test scores and other promised improvements failed to materialize, NCLB became a bipartisan cause once again, earning disapproval from both sides of the aisle in the 2010s. Among the conservative voices that have denounced NCLB, few have done so as dramatically or as forcefully as Diane Ravitch, whose public conversion from an NCLB supporter to an NCLB opponent rocked the world of education policy.[4]

Announcing her opposition to the world in a *Wall Street Journal* op-ed in March of 2010, Ravitch—a New York University professor of educational history—surprised the public and education experts alike.[5] Over the four previous decades, Ravitch had built a reputation as the arch-conservative of education scholarship.[6] With books like *The Revisionists Revised: A Critique of the Radical Attack on the Schools*, *The Troubled Crusade: American Education, 1945–1980*, and *Left Back: A Century of Failed School Reforms*, Ravitch had cultivated a conservative brand of education scholarship defending unfashionable policies like teaching the Western canon, the prioritization of achievement over equality, school choice, and even some early twentieth-century assimilationist policies.[7] In addition to writing a series of conservative-leaning histories, Ravitch served as assistant secretary for educational research in George H. W. Bush's Department of Education (ED).[8] During her time with the ED, Ravitch became an outspoken advocate for several education reforms favored by conservative policy makers, such as accountability and school choice. So, when she declared that NCLB was "disrupting communities, dumbing down our schools, giving students false reports of their progress, and creating a private sector that will undermine public education without improving it," many were shocked to learn that she had "changed [her] mind about the current direction of school reform."[9]

On the whole, Ravitch's conversion was received as a welcome addition to a political tide that had turned strongly against NCLB.[10] However, a small few did complain about Ravitch's change of heart, most notably Joel Klein, the former chancellor of the New York City Department of Education. In his memoir, Klein cast doubt on the sincerity of Ravitch's conversion by recounting a story about her partner, Mary Butz, a retired New York City school principal. Butz applied for a job as head of the New York City Leadership Academy, an elite administrative training program that prepares teachers and administrators to implement school reforms. According to Klein, Ravitch's public conversion was her reaction when Butz was passed over for the position.[11] Perhaps. But far more than just one scathing op-ed, Ravitch published two books, maintained a near daily blog on educational politics, and took her new point of view out onto the lecture circuit.[12] Her conversion has been—from all outward appearances—total and sustained. According to Ravitch, her evolution on NCLB had been brewing for some time when she finally announced it. A self-described iconoclast, Ravitch explained that outspokenly doubting the reform du jour—in this case NCLB—was a welcome return to the natural state of affairs for her.[13] Whatever happened to Diane Ravitch the private person, the change that has overcame Diane Ravitch the public figure is certifiable.

Treating Diane Ravitch as the definitive source on the educational politics of Diane Ravitch, this chapter takes a critical look at the rhetorical strategy of her conversion from NCLB supporter to NCLB detractor, but not along the sensationalistic lines that Klein's memoir has already covered.[14] Instead of trying to gauge her sincerity, I am interested in how

Ravitch made her conversion a moment of effective public persuasion. Ravitch has been an influential public intellectual on the subject of US education policy for decades. Although NCLB was not her idea, she played a prominent role in creating the climate of policy reform that ended in its passage.[15] As she announced her change of heart, Ravitch blamed NCLB not only for ruining public education, but also for duping her into supporting a reform agenda that promised results it could not deliver. In this way, Ravitch's public conversion employed blame not just to effect an overhaul of federal education policy, but also an overhaul of Diane Ravitch.

A conversion is a radical remaking of one's ethos that is meant to inspire others to either follow suit or reaffirm their faith.[16] In other words, a public conversion is, ideally, an act of civic leadership coincident with the renewal of the leader's civic identity. For Ravitch, this meant that her conversion had to account for her change of heart in a way that would not only permit her to continue as a credible public intellectual in education, but also rally others to her new cause. To account for how Ravitch achieved such an audacious rhetorical maneuver, I delve into her use of blame.

Endorsing a series of popular criticisms of NCLB—that it encouraged teaching to the test and cheating, narrowed the curriculum, and falsely reduced educational achievement to test scores—Ravitch focused her opposition to the law on the evils of accountability and the standardized testing industry. According to Ravitch and many others, NCLB's testing regime was mismeasuring educational quality and thereby hampering the national effort to improve the public schools. Defending all of the traditional hallmarks of privileged, suburban education that Adequate Yearly Progress (AYP) evaluations leave out—that good schools teach lifelong learners, have diverse curricula, and provide a variety of quality cocurricular activities—Ravitch blamed NCLB for distorting the distinction between successful and failing education. At the same time, Ravitch's reasons for blaming NCLB gave voice to a discomfort with the desegregation by category that resulted when AYP recategorized white working-class and rural schools—schools that many believed were succeeding—as failing. These schools were now being grouped with the urban black and Hispanic schools, which previously had by themselves defined failing education in the public mind. Through her defense of a traditional sense of what makes education successful, a sense that contrasts successful suburban schools and failing urban schools, Ravitch's blame for NCLB found a welcome reception, not just among a frustrated public, but in the words of President Barack Obama as he finally replaced the aged NCLB with the new Every Student Succeeds Act of 2015.

PUBLIC BLAME AND CONVERSION

A public conversion announces a change in the position and/or beliefs held by a political advocate to a mass audience. As such, a public conversion has two rhetorical tasks that it strives to achieve simultaneously: an overhaul of the advocate's ethos and the advocacy of a political position. Overhauling the advocate's ethos involves the convincing rationalization of a dramatic change of position in which the convert comes to inhabit a new character.[17] The simultaneous advocacy of a political position through conversion requires both rallying believers and appealing to potential converts. Public conversion is a volatile rhetorical process because the convert's advocacy of this new political position is the conversion, the shedding of his or her old political ethos. Persuading amid such uncertainty, an advocate engaged in public conversion risks having the trustworthiness of her words called into question, a prospect that threatens her ability to engage in politics.

To cope with the volatility of public conversion, advocates turn to strong words and even stronger rhetorical strategy. A public conversion can be effected through any number of rhetorical devices. However, because conversion involves a break with a past position, the juxtaposition between the new, corrected outlook and the old, broken position invites blame as an effective means of mediating between the two. An advocate engaged in public conversion must account convincingly for his or her change of heart, and blame provides a way of explaining that displaces fault away from the advocate, protecting her ability to speak effectively. All at once, the public act of blaming helps to remake the convert's ethos and rally support for his or her new cause.

The public performance of conversion has a history dating back at least as far as Emperor Constantine's famous decision to have his armies paint *Chi Rho* on their shields at the Battle of Milvian Bridge. As the story goes, the Christian God appeared to Constantine and his army and promised military victory in exchange for their artwork. However true or false that may be, Constantine won the battle and the story of his professed conversion to Christianity became a popular part of the history of the first Christian Emperor of Rome.[18] Although Emperor Constantine's tale of military conquest is no rhetorical model for Ravitch's public conversion, that even the emperor of Rome—possessing perhaps the most absolute power in all of human history—felt the need to give an explanation for changing his mind sheds some light on the delicacy of her situation.

Perhaps the best theoretical discussion of the relationship between rhetoric, ethos, and blameworthiness resides in the "Encomium of Helen," a speech in praise of Helen of Troy written by the sixth-century BCE sophist Gorgias of Leontini. In his encomium, Gorgias endeavored to "refute" the "crooked speech" of "those blaming Helen" for her role in instigating the Trojan War.[19] According to Gorgias, Helen's culpability depended on the circumstances under which she left Sparta to join Paris at Troy. Looking back at what was already a distant historical event, Gorgias did not so much praise Helen as dispute the blameworthiness of her actions. By addressing a series of scenarios, each potentially an explanation for her leaving, Gorgias argued that Helen was innocent on all counts. If, for example, it were the will of the gods, then her leaving was inevitable, "for the will of a god cannot be hindered by human forethought." If she "was abducted by force," Gorgias reasoned, then of course she was not to blame; likewise if she "was conquered by love." Finally, Gorgias argued at some length that "speech is a powerful lord." Therefore, "if persuasive discourse deceived her soul," we should "absolve [Helen] of responsibility."[20] For Gorgias, words held great power over people, so the condition of being persuaded was not blameworthy in much the same way as being moved by love, physical force, or the will of the gods.

Although Gorgias sought to "remove infamy from a woman" by absolving Helen of blame for the Trojan War, his rhetorical strategy required him to also place blame as a means of substitution.[21] In each case, Gorgias replaced Helen with some other, better candidate for blame, be it human, god, emotion, or the power of language itself. In this sense, Gorgias's speech was ironic: a speech against blame that embraced blame as its principal argumentative strategy. This core contradiction does not mean that the speech failed its purpose; it is widely recognized as a great historical speech. But it does highlight how difficult it is to avoid blame when attempting to remake one's ethos. In this way, the "Encomium of Helen" provides a model for Ravitch's public conversion. Like Gorgias, Ravitch spoke in the pursuit of exoneration and also blamed powerful words, in the form of the NCLB, for persuading her soul.

A DECEPTIVE, PERSUASIVE LAW

On March 9, 2010, a week after the release of her latest book, *The Death and Life of the Great American School System*, Diane Ravitch published an op-ed in the *Wall Street Journal* declaring that she had changed her mind about education policy. In the first three paragraphs, Ravitch reviewed her conservative bona fides, then turned to the issue at hand:

> As No Child Left Behind's (NCLB) accountability regime took over the nation's schools under President George W. Bush and more and more charter schools were launched, I supported these initiatives. But over time, I became disillusioned with the strategies that once seemed so promising. I no longer believe that either approach will produce the quantum improvement in American education that we all hope for.[22]

After nearly four decades of conservative scholarship, two of which she spent actively promoting the research and implementation of school choice and accountability, Ravitch had changed her mind about what was best for the public schools. No longer would she support charter schooling or accountability as the best policy solutions for declining achievement and swelling inequality. Stating her opinion in characteristically blunt terms, Ravitch declared that accountability had "turned into a nightmare for American schools."[23] The harshly worded op-ed was, in part, an advertisement for her new book, but it also began the process of accounting for why Ravitch had undergone such a dramatic change in perspective.

In *The Death and Life of the Great American School System*, Ravitch expanded the conversation from the *Wall Street Journal* op-ed. Laying out the case for her new point of view on education policy, she began with the story of how she came to see things differently—that is, the story of her conversion. "In the fall of 2007, I reluctantly decided to have my office repainted," Ravitch recalled. Through the "pleasantly ruminative" chore of packing and unpacking "twenty years of papers and books," Ravitch explained that she found herself confronted with an "intellectual crisis." This crisis led to a "wrenching transformation in my perspective on school reform," she revealed. "Where once I had been hopeful, even enthusiastic, about the potential benefits of testing, accountability, choice, and markets," she said, "I now found myself experiencing profound doubts."[24] As she continued, Ravitch explained that she began to change her mind as the better educational outcomes NCLB had promised to her and the country failed to materialize despite more than five years of tests and reforms under the new law. Although NCLB was "surrounded with a great deal of high-flown rhetoric when it was passed, promising a new era of high standards and high accomplishments," Ravitch eventually concluded that "the reality was far different. Its remedies did not work."[25] NCLB had deceived her with its rhetoric, promising a future it did not deliver.

Seeking persuasion through public conversion, Ravitch needed to reconstruct her ethos in such a way that her argument about the failures of NCLB would be taken seriously. Given NCLB's broad unpopularity, this might sound like a fairly simple task, but Ravitch had—by her own admission—advocated many of the reforms at the core of NCLB. Her change of heart begged several important questions. If she had been wrong before, why should she be trusted now? Was this newfound skepticism a cynical bid to join the winning team? What had changed her mind? Were her reasons defensible? To address these and other doubts about the trustworthiness of her new advocacy, Ravitch needed to provide an explanation for the personal transformation that resulted in her public conversion. In her introduction to *The Death and Life of the Great American School System*, Ravitch seemed keenly aware of the difficult position her conversion had created, asking herself aloud: "Was it like me to shuffle off ideas like an ill-fitting coat?" Ravitch answered her own question in the negative by once again reviewing her career. According to the personal assessment she performed while packing and unpacking her office, "one constant" in her academic and political writing was a "skepticism about pedagogical fads, enthusiasms, and movements."[26] Indeed, Ravitch identified "the conflict between promise and reality" as a "constant preoccupation" in her academic work, stretching all the way back to her first journal article in 1968.[27] Although she had experienced a conversion on the questions of school choice and accountability, such dramatic changes did not typify her ethos as an academic and public figure. So, what did?

Accounting for her conversion, Ravitch tackled the problem of reconstructing her ethos by characterizing her support of NCLB as the culmination of a long, unfortunate deviation from her usual habit of making good judgments about education policy, grounded in the generous application of skepticism and doubt. Throughout *The Death and Life of the Great American School System*, Ravitch blamed NCLB for the failures of public education reform during the 2000s. But, as she explained her conversion in the introduction, Ravitch also blamed NCLB for fooling her into abandoning her skepticism and supporting the law. According to Ravitch, NCLB overcame her doubts by deception. Recounting the return of her doubtfulness, Ravitch confessed:

> I realized, I was turning skeptical in response to panaceas and miracle cures. The only difference was that in this case, I too had fallen for the latest panaceas and miracle cures; I too had drunk deeply of the elixir that promised a quick fix to intractable problems. I too had jumped aboard the bandwagon, one festooned with banners celebrating the power of accountability, incentive, and markets. I too was captivated by these ideals.[28]

In comparing the persuasive power of the accountability and school choice policies written into NCLB to that of an elixir, Ravitch—perhaps unwittingly—employed a metaphor made famous by Gorgias's "Encomium of Helen." In his attempt to exonerate Helen on the grounds that she could not be held responsible if she had been persuaded to leave Sparta for Troy, Gorgias observed that "the power of discourse stands in the same relation to the soul's organization as the pharmacopoeia does to the physiology of bodies." Gorgias also warned that some such discourses "by a certain vile persuasion drug can trick the soul."[29] For Gorgias, words persuade the mind in much the same way that drugs affect the body; they elicit an involuntary response. Thus, like a patient under the influence of a drug, a person under the influence of persuasion cannot be held fully accountable for his or her actions. According to Ravitch, NCLB was an example of what Gorgias called a "vile persuasion drug"—deft policy language deceiving her like a sort of rhetorical narcotic. Providing her own account of the events of the 1990s and 2000s, Ravitch more or less admitted that NCLB had been a bad idea from the start, but that she had been helpless to resist its persuasiveness because NCLB was not just any policy proposal—it was a fad.

When discussing NCLB and school choice, Ravitch used the term *fad*. According to Ravitch, fads are treacherous because they possess the capacity to deceive people. In the world of education policy, fads usually appear as reforms that are too good to be true. They are predicated on false promises and false hope. Despite—or perhaps because—they overpromise and oversimplify education policy, fads attain broad popularity. Through their popularity, fads achieve mass persuasion and the implementation of the reforms they prescribe. Ravitch warned that fads can be oppressive, persuading not only by the intimidating force of their popularity, but also by force alone. In the case of NCLB, Ravitch observed that "many educators have their doubts about the slogans and cure-alls of our time, but they are required to follow the mandates of federal law (such as No Child Left Behind) despite their doubts."[30] Although Ravitch—an elite university professor—was never subject to the requirements or the consequences of NCLB, her example of the law's ability to conquer doubt by force helped characterize her opposition to a law as an ethical decision. Even though she had lent her influence to the creation and implementation of NCLB, the newly converted Ravitch stood against the law in the name of those educators it deceived and oppressed when it quashed their doubts.

By characterizing NCLB as a deceptive law emerging from the accountability fad, both Ravitch's initial embrace and later rejection of NCLB were cast, not as the waffling of an uncertain or disingenuous advocate, but as the faultless actions of an imperfect, but well-meaning skeptic. Thus, by denouncing her former advocacy for NCLB, Ravitch was not detracting from her ethos, but actually enhancing it. Able to see her "way through the blind assumptions of ideology and politics," Ravitch reconfirmed her identity as a hard-nosed education scholar willing to act on her vision regardless of the consequences, countervailing popular opinion, or even the need for her to admit that she had been wrong.[31] Realizing her mistake and professing her awe at the power of persuasion, like Gorgias did on behalf of Helen, Ravitch presented herself as brave, but also humble enough to admit her error in order to move forward. In addition, she offered her readers an account of her purportedly true self, the one who should have known better all along and that she returned to by rejecting NCLB. This true self, a trustworthy teller of difficult truths, was to be believed instead of the Diane Ravitch of the 1990s and 2000s. Reflecting on this moment of self-discovery, Ravitch explained that she realized she was "'too conservative' to embrace an agenda whose end result [was] entirely speculative and uncertain."[32] In other words, Ravitch concluded that rejecting NCLB was what she should have done all along.

Ravitch bolstered her trustworthiness by reasoning aloud through her changed perspective on education policy, but also by broadcasting her anguish with the process of conversion. In the introduction to *The Death and Life of the Great American Schools System*, Ravitch talked through some of the self-doubt brought on by her conversion, making it clear to her audience that she took no pleasure in the process. "I have a right to change my mind. Fair enough," she posed, "but why, I kept wondering, why had I changed my mind?"[33] Answering her own question, Ravitch explained: "My views changed as I saw how these ideas were working out in reality."[34] For Ravitch, the process of conversion was not a welcome eureka moment. Instead, like her initial deception by the NCLB fad, her conversion was brought about by outside forces that caused her to realize that she should have known better. Observing NCLB fail to live up to her expectations left Ravitch no choice, rationalizing her change of heart and estranging her from the agency that might make her blameworthy. In particular, Ravitch pointed to an evolution of "the facts" as NCLB's promised gains in test scores and educational quality failed to materialize.[35] As she succinctly put it in the first chapter, "I saw my hopes for better education turn into a measurement strategy."[36] This unfortunate development, which she characterizes as outside of her control and against her intentions, ultimately set into motion the events that led to her conversion. Ravitch's politics merely reflected these developments and the underlying consistency of her fact-based approach to education policy. When the best information available pointed in a new direction, so did she: mistaken and therefore inconsistent, but honest and therefore blameless.

BLAMING NO CHILD LEFT BEHIND

In *The Death and Life of the Great American School System*, not only did Ravitch declare her change of mind, but she chose to do so for a popular audience, making her conversion both public and part of a larger act of advocacy. After the introduction to *The Death and Life of the Great American School System*, Ravitch left almost all questions about her conversion behind to make her case for policy change.[37] Consequently, the vast majority of the book is a lengthy and detailed polemic against the NCLB era of federal education policy. This made sense. On the one hand, the breadth and depth of Ravitch's argument against NCLB substantiated her conversion. A law so bad as the one she described over the following two hundred and seventy plus pages deserved no one's support, least of all the author of such a thorough and uncompromising takedown. On the other hand, her merciless discrediting of the policy reforms she had originally helped to champion redirected blame from herself, as one of the policy elites who helped bring about NCLB, to the law itself. In the process, Ravitch voiced her support for a series of popular criticisms of NCLB, all of which were predicated on the same discomfort with the persuasive power of words she blamed for leading her to mistakenly support school choice and accountability in the 1990s and 2000s. According to Ravitch, NCLB's tricky language made it successful as a fad, but ensured its failure as a policy.

Ravitch's argument against NCLB was expansive and as a result her book included discussions of a host of issues aside from the problems of NCLB itself. From an insider's history of the evolution of accountability and school choice policy to a scathing indictment of the standardized testing industry, Ravitch ranged across the landscape of education policy in the twilight of the NCLB era. However, her effort to blame NCLB for the failures of education policy during the 2000s had a core set of arguments, all grounded in the problems of standardized testing. The requirement that states use standardized tests to measure educational success and failure was the chief innovation distinguishing NCLB from previous versions of the ESEA. Thus, Ravitch's decision to use standardized testing as the anchor linking NCLB to a series of bad policy outcomes was a sound argumentative strategy. According to Ravitch, the problems with NCLB all stemmed from this core policy innovation. Of course, by 2010 the argument against NCLB's testing regime was already familiar to anyone who had taken an interest in the public discussion of education policy over the previous decade. Few were likely to pick up Ravitch's book and read for the first time that NCLB was, for example, narrowing the curriculum, but they might have been surprised to discover that Ravitch now believed that it did. Thus, an additional benefit to Ravitch's decision to critique NCLB on the grounds that its testing requirements had damaged public education was that she did not have to invent new lines of argument, so much as lend her support to several well-established positions.

Although Ravitch discussed a number of problems with NCLB's testing regime, such as the predatory role of the testing industry and the way high-stakes testing encouraged teachers to teach to the test, in her view the various dysfunctions of testing all led to two related outcomes: narrowed curricula and a distorted conception of what constitutes a good education. Ravitch began her argument about the narrowing of curricula early in *The Death and Life of the Great American School System* by telling the story of New York School District 2 in the 1990s. Considered a great success story and a model for the sort of school reforms that NCLB envisioned, District 2 underwent a dramatic reform of its reading curriculum, in which a great deal of the school district's curricular focus was shifted from other priorities toward reading. "Large blocks of time," Ravitch explained, were "set aside each day for literacy instruction, in which children engage in structured activities such as shared reading, guided reading, independent reading, word study, writing, and reading aloud."[38] Called "Balanced Literacy," this new reading curriculum was, according to Ravitch, one of the instructional fads that first inspired and then came to typify NCLB reforms. Following some of the key figures of Balanced Literacy, Ravitch traced its implementation across the country. Ravitch quoted one San Diego kindergarten teacher who described the massive reading blocks required by Balanced Literacy as "the monster to which we fed our kids."[39] Even before the passage of NCLB, Balanced Literacy was unbalancing public school curricula.

For Ravitch, the problem with Balanced Literacy and its similarly draconian mathematical counterparts was not necessarily that they were failed curricula, but that they tended to take over the school. Because NCLB tested student progress only in math and reading (later adding science), schools pursued those subjects to the detriment of others, argued Ravitch. Returning to the subject of New York City's public schools, Ravitch discussed the New York City Department of Education's reform efforts under Joel Klein in the 2000s. According to Ravitch, the department's focus on reading and mathematics led to a decline of arts education. By 2009, she noted, nearly one third of schools had no art teacher.[40] Also, over that same period, Ravitch observed that test scores in subjects other than math and reading declined.[41] Finally, Ravitch concluded that "a lack of attention to history, science, and the arts detracts from the quality of education, the quality of children's lives, the quality of daily life in school, and even performance on the tests."[42] In other words, the result of NCLB was a narrowed curriculum, an outcome that Ravitch argued was bad in and of itself, because the kind of education it required created poorer-quality citizens. Ravitch preferred the breadth of the liberal education that typified public education in the United States during the latter half of the twentieth century.

Ravitch was not alone in feeling this way. Before the passage of NCLB, successful schools were understood to create good outcomes for their students, like high test scores and admission to prestigious colleges, but they were also understood to achieve those outcomes by providing a great many resources for a broad array of educational opportunities. Recall that when Jonathan Kozol, in *Savage Inequalities*, was comparing schools in

New York, Chicago, and elsewhere to argue that they were unequal, his evidence rested in part on per-pupil expenditures because these allowed for the provision of fancy resources like PS 24's on-campus planetarium and New Trier High School's seven gyms. A wide array of resources in a wide array of subjects was a crucial part of what marked a successful school from a failing one. Kozol's canonical work of educational criticism made little mention of test scores. Regardless of whether planetariums or an embarrassment of gymnasia were correlated with higher test scores—and they probably were—their existence on a public school campus was taken to be an indication of a high quality of education.

Aside from the other proxies people used to distinguish good schools from bad ones, indicators like the racial and class makeup of the school and its surrounding community, and its ability or inability to provide a broad curriculum, helped make that distinction. Both Kozol and Ravitch argued that the presence of opportunities like Advanced Placement or Latin courses or clubs for music, advanced math, chess, debate, or even astronomy were good indicators of the quality of education available at a given school. NCLB's privileging of remedial math and reading reforms turned this previous assumption on its head. Instead of commending as successful those schools that provided a broad curriculum fostering each student's varied interests, NCLB tended to reward and celebrate schools that eschewed a broad approach to schooling in favor of a narrow focus on proficiency in the fundamental subjects of math and reading. Not only did this offend Ravitch, but it also struck a blow at the common assumption that white rural and working-class schools—places with music, sports, 4-H, and so on—were producing superior citizens as compared to poorer urban schools with narrower ranges of curricular opportunities. By encouraging and, in some cases, requiring the narrowing of school curriculums, NCLB had undercut how Americans distinguish between the successful and failed production of future citizens.[43] Wisely, Ravitch rested much of her argument on the unpopularity of this realignment. For Ravitch, the problem with NCLB was once again its ability to persuade educators and policy makers to abandon their previously good judgment, convincing them not just to narrow curricula, but also to view the consequences of a narrow curriculum as preferable.

In addition to narrowing the curriculum and producing inferior citizens, Ravitch argued that with its focus on testing, NCLB had distorted the difference between successful and failing education, changing the stakes of schooling from the production of citizens to the production of test scores. To make this argument Ravitch contended that standardized tests were ill-equipped to measure the successes or failures of an entire school. She also argued that the high stakes NCLB put on standardized tests guaranteed that those tests would measure only the degree to which a particular teacher or school had committed themselves to achieving a good score, not the true quality of the education they provided.

Throughout *The Death and Life of the Great American School System*, Ravitch rehearsed many familiar arguments about the inadequacies of standardized tests. For example, she argued that standardized tests lacked the precision to aid in decisions on an individual level. "Tests are not precise instruments," Ravitch exclaimed; they do not "have scientific validity, like that of a thermometer or barometer."[44] "The trouble with test-based accountability," she continued, "is that it imposes serious consequences on children, educators, and schools on the basis of test scores that may reflect measurement error, statistical error, random variation, or a host of environmental factors or student attributes. None of us would want to be evaluated—with our reputation and livelihood on the line—solely on the basis of an instrument that is prone to error and ambiguity."[45] For Ravitch, the leap from test outcome to policy response was too great. With too much noise feeding into the production of test scores, policy makers had no way to be sure whether the reforms they implemented in response were actually addressing the real causes of inadequate test scores.

In addition to the imprecision of standardized testing, Ravitch argued that the high stakes of the AYP process encouraged educational practices that distorted the outcomes of testing. "Test preparation," she explained, is the "most common" way of "gaming the system." According to Ravitch, rearranging the school day to include excessive test practice could ensure higher scores while actually damaging the school's quality of education. "The consequence of all this practice is that students may be able to pass the state test, yet unable to pass a test of precisely the same subject for which they did not practice."[46] In the end, Ravitch noted that "excessive test preparation distorts the very purpose of tests, which is to assess learning and knowledge, not just to produce higher test scores."[47] In this way, she argued, test preparation not only distorted the test's ability to measure the comparative quality of education between districts, schools, students, and teachers, but it also introduced a distortion into the classroom, where what counts as meaningful education is truncated to just those things that help students prepare for tests. Test preparation, Ravitch feared, had taken precedence over the preparation of citizens.

Overall, Ravitch argued that high-stakes standardized tests distorted not only the public's understanding of which schools were succeeding or failing, but also how that distinction ought to be made. Once again Ravitch returned to the example of the New York City public schools. Lamenting the school report card system the city used, a system that assigned grades based on the rise and fall of average test scores, Ravitch wrote:

> Some excellent schools, known for their sense of community and consistently high scores, received an F because their scores dipped a few points. Some very low-performing schools, even some the State Education Department ranked as persistently dangerous, received an A because they showed some improvement.[48]

According to Ravitch, this "obsession" over test scores overshadowed the true purpose of schooling—to produce good citizens.[49] In essence, NCLB's testing regime, meant to prevent Americans from ignoring the parts of their public education system that were failing, had actually further mystified the difference between good and bad schools. Worse still, NCLB had inspired local educational administrators like Klein to engage in public discourse that was participating in this mystification. Just as Ravitch was deceived by the policy-making fads that resulted in the passage of NCLB, so did the new law deceive other educational leaders and present a false account of the purpose of education to the public. Fortunately for the converting Ravitch, her argument against NCLB seemed to confirm that she was not alone in being fooled by the law.

At the end of the *Wall Street Journal* op-ed where she publicly announced her conversion, Ravitch delivered a call for action summarizing the grievances she detailed in *The Death and Life of the Great American School System*:

> What we need is not a marketplace, but a coherent curriculum that prepares all students. And our government should commit to providing a good school in every neighborhood in the nation, just as we strive to provide a good fire company in every community.
>
> On our present course, we are disrupting communities, dumbing down our schools, giving students false reports of their progress, and creating a private sector that will undermine public education without improving it. Most significantly, we are not producing a generation of students who are more knowledgeable, and better prepared for the responsibilities of citizenship. That is why I changed my mind about the current direction of school reform.[50]

For Ravitch, NCLB's regime of market-based school reforms effected through high-stakes standardized testing was ruining public education in America. But even more concerning than the effects of the policy as it was implemented was its ability to maintain so much support for its cause. Once again, few readers of Ravitch's book would have been surprised to learn about the deleterious effects of NCLB. What made Ravitch's denunciation novel, if not entirely unique, was her stand against the persuasive power of the law, a stand necessitated by her need to account for her conversion by blaming NCLB.

THE RHETORICAL LEGACY OF A POWERFUL CONVERSION

In order to advocate for policy change while simultaneously accounting for her sudden change of position from an NCLB supporter to one of its harshest critics, Diane Ravitch blamed NCLB both for her deceiving her and for harming the public schools during the 2000s. Presented as an explanation for her mistaken decision to support NCLB in the introduction to *The Death and Life of the Great American School System*, Ravitch's assertion that NCLB was a deceptive law born of the accountability fad turns out to also be her underpinning explanation of how NCLB did so much damage to American public education. Through the high-stakes testing of reading and math, NCLB not only narrowed school curricula, but also misused testing data to convince many educators and policy makers that a narrowed curriculum constituted the best path to educational progress. By reducing public education to the pursuit of test scores, Ravitch argued that NCLB distorted the meaning of education itself, abandoning its civic mission.

This broad discomfort with the persuasive power of NCLB as a public policy helped to exonerate Ravitch from her role in bringing the law about. Like Gorgias's Helen, Ravitch was carried away by forces beyond her control. By blaming NCLB for deceiving her, a self-declared skeptic of just the sort of overpromising reform the law turned out to be, Ravitch attributed a great deal of rhetorical agency to NCLB, just like many frustrated parents and educators who resented the failing label NCLB gave to so many previously well-regarded schools. Because of the law's universal proficiency requirement, the failure to meet AYP proved to be a statistical inevitability for the vast majority of public schools.[51] In this sense, NCLB's failing label was meaningless, more a function of federal law than a reflection of the quality of education at a given school. Nonetheless, the fear that NCLB's label held broad persuasive power—that others might now regard as failing a school previously considered successful—underpinned much of the preexisting public dislike of NCLB before Ravitch's conversion.[52] The white working- and middle-class parents sending their children to suburban and rural schools were, like Ravitch, spooked by the power of language—in their case, to issue a broad and persuasive decree that the schools they assumed to be superior to urban black and Hispanic schools were actually failing educationally in equivalent ways. By attacking NCLB for abusing its power of persuasion, Ravitch gave voice to the fears of a broader constituency that already worried that NCLB might take away their access to good education, not by implementation of policy, but by a policy of reclassification.

Explaining why she had to make her conversion public in *The Death and Life of the Great American School System*, Ravitch observed: "We as a society cannot extricate ourselves from fads and nostrums unless we carefully look at how we got entangled in them." According to Ravitch, NCLB was the fad, and she "needed to explain why" she "had returned" to her "roots as a partisan of the American public education."[53] Pitting herself on the side of public education and blaming NCLB not just for harming it, but for deceiving herself and many others into believing that the law would help public education, Ravitch provided a rhetorical model for others who wanted to change their own positions. Admitting the mistaken nature of her support for NCLB, but maintaining that the law deserved the preponderance of the blame for the educational failures of the 2000s, Ravitch made clever use of blame to effect a public conversion in which she was able to maintain the ethos of a trustworthy advocate and to mount a call for conversion. She could no longer stand by as NCLB deceived policy makers and educators and damaged the schools, and neither should others.

The legacy of Ravitch's spectacular conversion can be observed in the passage of the Every Student Succeeds Act of 2015 (ESSA). Formally ending NCLB, the ESSA devolved some control over the accountability process to the states, a policy outcome that had effectively begun through waivers already in use when Ravitch announced her conversion. Whether the ESSA proves a significant change in the policy of public education in the United States or simply amounts to NCLB-lite remains to be seen. However, the change in the public discussion of education policy portended by Ravitch's conversion was already apparent by the time the new law was passed. For example, upon signing the ESSA into law, President Barack Obama took the opportunity to reflect on the legacy of NCLB:

> The goals of No Child Left Behind, the predecessor of this law, were the right ones: High standards. Accountability. Closing the achievement gap. Making sure that every child was learning, not just some. But in practice, it often fell short. It didn't always consider the specific needs of each community. It led to too much testing during classroom time. It often forced schools and school districts into cookie-cutter reforms that didn't always produce the kinds of results that we wanted to see.[54]

The similarities between Obama's remarks and Ravitch's criticisms of NCLB are remarkable. Obama listed many of the same problems Ravitch discussed at length in *The Death and Life of the Great American School System*. NCLB hurt schools by upsetting them at the community level, required too much testing, distorted the curriculum by encouraging an excess of test preparation, and required reforms based on those mistaken conceptions of what makes good and bad education. However, Obama's remarks not only mimicked the content of Ravitch's critique, they also mimicked its form. The president observed that although NCLB made the "right" promises, it still "fell short." Just like Ravitch's remarks in her public conversion, Obama lamented NCLB's false promises. The chief problem with NCLB was its deceptive use of language.

In this way, Ravitch's public conversion opened space for a new blame narrative. Instead of the accountability narrative that insisted on the scapegoating of educators and administrators for the failures of public education, Ravitch, in her conversion, helped make it okay to blame education reform itself.[55] According to this new narrative, NCLB made false promises, fooling Ravitch and others into supporting those ill-advised "cookie-cutter reforms" President Obama spoke of regretfully as he replaced the aged law. When NCLB ultimately failed to live up to the promises it made for a better educational future, the law itself became the target of the blame narrative it was designed to harness. However, now that NCLB has been replaced, its days as the chief target of public blame in the rhetoric of education policy are surely numbered.

6

The Paradox of Public Blame: A History of US Education Policy

Since the founding of the Department of Education (ED), the national discussion of education policy has resounded with public blame. Although it was not free of blame before President Jimmy Carter reorganized the executive branch in October of 1979, the prominence, prevalence, and potency of blame has certainly increased.[1] As the national discussion Carter invited when he founded the ED has taken hold, blame has come to the fore as a chief means by which Americans dispute the future of their public schools. If nothing else, the preceding case studies demonstrate the indispensability of blame for the most impactful acts of advocacy in the world of education policy from 1979 to the present. Individually, the rhetorical successes and failures of each case are illuminated by following the use of blame and asking how each advocate employed the art of public accusation. However, if the intensification of public blaming is indeed a discernable trend, then an examination of it across three decades of public discourse should also reveal some cumulative consequences with repercussions for the whole of education policy.

Both this chapter and the next range back over the case studies, synthesizing their findings in order to describe the cumulative effects of blame on public discussion of education policy. What I call the "paradox of public blame" gives form to these two syntheses. The paradox is as such. On the one hand, public blame expresses and therefore relies upon a great deal of civic faith. Each act of public blaming is a bid for hearts and minds. When a reform advocate uses public blame, she calls others to see a problem and its cause in the same way that she does. She also asks, implicitly if not explicitly, those who agree to join her in taking action to remedy the problem. In attempting to persuade her fellow citizens, her act of public advocacy assumes that the better argument can ultimately carry the day, resulting in policy change. By sharing her concerns despite the risk of public rebuke, an advocate who employs public blame takes a profoundly civic action, one that breathes life and consequence into deliberation.

On the other hand, public blame is often perceived as a sign that the deliberation in which it appears has lost credibility. Blame, especially when it participates in a larger trend of blaming, can come across as cynical or perfunctory, a rhetorical strategy devoid of the genuine concern that would make it a meaningful civic act. In such cases, public blame can be perceived as a rhetorical power play, an attempt to manipulate the public, rather than persuade it. Importantly, though, the consequences of transparently dubious public blame extend beyond the credibility and persuasiveness of the advocate who engaged in it. The abuse of blame degrades the credibility and persuasiveness of the entire deliberation in which it appears—at its extreme, making meaningful deliberation impossible. So, paradoxically, the use of blaming as public advocacy can undermine the same civic faith in the legitimacy of deliberation upon which the persuasive power of public blame is predicated.[2]

Throughout the remainder of this chapter, I argue that this loss of credibility and persuasiveness is precisely what has been happening to the public discussion of education policy in the United States. For evidence, one need look no further than the pessimism that abounds in education scholarship. Then, in the next chapter, I discuss some ways public blame can be reconfigured in the hopes of restoring contemporary education policy's deficit of civic faith.

PUBLIC BLAME, A RHETORICAL CONSENSUS

The scholarly discussion of public education has taken a dark turn over the past decade. From a debate over whether public education exists in a state of crisis, scholars have turned their attention to the question of whether the crisis, now largely undisputed, is in fact existential.[3] Two camps have emerged, and neither paints a rosy picture of the prospects for education policy. One group of scholars doubts whether public education can, does, or has ever existed outside the cycles of crisis and reform.[4] For these scholars, the problems with public education are baked into history and institutional structure in such a way that undoing them is, at minimum, a project of generational proportions. Another group of scholars rejects the idea that public education in the United States is fatally flawed, but also sees it as less institutionally stable. In a policy-making context that doubts the effectiveness of public educators and the institutions that employ them, these scholars worry whether the nationwide system of public schools established throughout the late nineteenth and early twentieth century will long endure.[5] For them, there is the real prospect that public education as we know it might be reformed or legislated out of existence.

Both groups of scholars agree that public education exists in an endless state of reform, and that the present trend is for reforms to be increasingly directed by entities from the private sector. For example, since the passage of No Child Left Behind (NCLB), charter schools have claimed broad gains in many of the nation's largest cities, including Milwaukee, Detroit, New Orleans, Chicago, and Washington, DC, where they now make up a considerable percentage of the schools.[6] Along with the growth of charter schooling, the rise of the standardized testing industry and the increasing popularity of homeschooling have all contributed to the privatization of American education.

A close look at the use of blame in the rhetoric of education policy over the past thirty-five years does little to dispel these concerns. It does, however, shed additional light on the rise of accountability politics in education. Some scholars, such as Jal Mehta, have argued that accountability's policy successes in the 1990s resulted from the bipartisan appeal of making new policies that would get more out of existing institutions by holding officials to account.[7] However, in addition to benefiting from a bipartisan political consensus, accountability has profited from a bipartisan rhetorical consensus. Whether liberal, conservative, old left, new right, neoliberal, or neo-Marxist, advocates of all stripes can be found employing public blame as they debate education policy. Indeed, public blame is employed by public education's supporters just as often as its detractors, and this trend shows no signs of abating, even in the emerging post-NCLB era. Importantly, though, public blame is not a policy-neutral rhetorical strategy. By constantly casting doubt on the educational status quo, public blame manufactures a need for greater traction between policy decisions and educational outcomes. This concern with the issue of policy implementation is the core justification for accountability-based policies. Despite this inherent bias, public blame is often employed by advocates who oppose high-stakes standardized testing, school choice, and other policies that are supposed to improve public education by making educators and schools more accountable for educational outcomes. This rhetorical consensus that education policy advocacy begins with public blame helps explain how even those opposed to accountability have inadvertently contributed to its rise.

For other scholars, including Diane Ravitch, the success of accountability is a more partisan phenomenon, a favorable policy strategy employed by skilled policy advocates on the right ultimately interested in accelerating the corporatization of education. I am not so generous as to credit policy advocates in the 1980s and 1990s with the forethought to choose a rhetorical strategy commensurate with a long-term interest in privatization, which really coevolved with that strategy. However, the consensus around the rhetoric of public blame has proven helpful for the cause of privatization beyond the political consensus it helped to sustain around accountability. In addition to contriving a felt need for accountability, public blame has also helped to create a rancorous and often dysfunctional deliberation over education policy that casts doubt over the wisdom of pursuing education as a public enterprise. When arguments over public policy exacerbate divisions between groups of Americans, stressing their incompatibility, the very idea of an education system meant to serve the needs of everyone begins to look like a bad policy goal. In this way, the rhetorical consensus around public blame does indeed pose an existential threat to public education.

PUBLIC BLAME AND THE RISE OF ACCOUNTABILITY

To explain public blame's role in the rise of accountability, a review of the case studies is instructive. On its face, Milton Friedman's public use of blame to argue that unaccountable bureaucrats—typically in the form of school principals and district employees—were ruining the public schools was meant to serve as evidence for the superiority of school choice. Friedman used public blame to argue that public education was failing to provide a high-quality service due to a lack of free market competition. His solution was to make educators more beholden to the preferences of parents, who would shop around for schools, treating their children's education as any other privately purchased service. In addition, though, Friedman's use of public blame as an *ad hominem* attack discredited his debate opponents on the grounds that they were too invested in the public system of education to have trustworthy opinions about the prospects of education policies that incorporated private sector solutions. Because public blame asserts that public education is failing its charge in a way that confers culpability on whoever is responsible for that failure, it also asserts a need to hold accountable those who are deemed culpable. In Friedman's case, this justified discounting the arguments of the experts he invited to debate the merits of school choice, making for an impressive spectacle where Friedman appeared to singlehandedly defeat a team of education experts with savvy economic analysis. Thus, in the case of Friedman's *Free to Choose* television series, public blame made a powerful appeal for accountability and privatization, but admittedly, by design.

In its influential report, *A Nation at Risk: The Imperative for Educational Reform*, the National Commission on Excellence in Education (NCEE) used public blame to call, above all else, for the pursuit of higher educational standards. Throughout *A Nation at Risk*, the NCEE made it clear that the state of public education in the United States in the early 1980s was unacceptable, and that the country had no one to blame but itself. Educational failure, according to the report, was the result of a simple loss of the will to do better, a collective decline of expectations. The NCEE's act of self-blame proved epochal, securing the place of educational achievement as the primary goal of educational policy making, even above the pursuit of greater equality.[8] Even Friedman, just a few years earlier, had taken time to hedge his bets by arguing that school choice had the potential to help equalize access to a higher quality of education for poor families. As I have argued, *A Nation at Risk*'s remarkable influence on the education policy that has followed it resulted in part from the NCEE's clever use of self-blame, a rhetorical strategy that allowed it to both place and accept blame for the failures of US public education. The result of such successful public blame has been to fix policy makers on the goal of increasing educational achievement, but also to discredit education policyspeak that does not begin with the assertion that public education is, in some dramatic way, inadequate at a systemic level. In the wake of *A Nation at Risk*, public education has had few public figures willing to speak positively on its behalf. Instead, successful policy advocacy most often begins by presenting a tale of educational failure, demonstrating that the policy advocate shares the unflinchingly critical perspective on public education presented in *A Nation at Risk.*

For example, although Jonathan Kozol opposed excellence as the chief goal of education policy, his contributions to the discussion of education policy in the early 1990s appealed to the nation's sense of shame, much like *A Nation at Risk.* A holdover from the era of access, Kozol argued for greater educational equity in *Savage Inequalities: Children in America's Schools.* According to Kozol, the best way for the United States to improve its schools was for it to finish the work of desegregating them. However, to make this argument convincingly, especially after the NCEE had raised the issue of public education to a matter of national security, Kozol needed to present a strong exigency for policy change. To do so, he devoted most of his book to chronicling the failures of the public education system in those places where it most needed to succeed. Comparing majority white and majority minority schools across the country, *Savage Inequalities* vividly illustrated the unfairness of the quality of education available to Americans from different racial and ethnic backgrounds through tales of grinding poverty and egregious institutional failures. Although Kozol favored desegregation as a policy solution over the equalization of funding or even the pursuit of higher academic standards, and although he sympathized with the plight of both students and educators in poor school districts, the narrative of educational failure in *Savage Inequalities* still lent itself to a growing push for greater accountability. Despite Kozol's explicit advocacy of desegregation, *Savage Inequalities* was received as more evidence of just how bad public education had become. Blaming segregation for the failures of public education through gripping depictions of racial inequality, Kozol's portrayal of educational failure did not refute, but instead merely diversified *A Nation at Risk*'s call for accountability.

This diversification of the call for greater accountability is reflected in NCLB's insistence that public education must make all children proficient in reading and math.[9] Incorporating the narrative of educational failure from the likes of Kozol and other social reformers, President George W.

Bush campaigned for greater accountability in public education as a way of addressing the "soft bigotry of low expectations."[10] Although Bush and Kozol advocated different policy solutions, their descriptions of what ailed public education were not so different. When Bush insisted over and over again that "every child can learn," he did so to clarify his position against the systemic racism that Kozol depicted in *Savage Inequalities*.[11] Through the logic of compassionate conservatism, the stereotype of the dangerously underperforming public school destroying the futures of children in poor and urban settings became yet another justification for accountability. By embracing a bipartisan narrative that blamed the pubic schools for failing to provide an adequate education to America's most underprivileged children, NCLB shifted responsibility for educational success and failure away from parents and legislators and onto teachers and school administrators, the street-level bureaucrats of public education. Once written into law by the reauthorization of the Elementary and Secondary Education Act of 1965 (ESEA) as NCLB, the political consensus that blamed educational failure on underperforming schools proved so effective that it made NCLB the longest-reigning reauthorization in the history of the ESEA. After two decades of public blame from the left, the right, and the center, it seemed that the entirety of the American electorate had been ready for legislation that would, more than anything else, hold someone accountable.

Of course, the consensus NCLB presided over was anything but homogenous. Many educators and activists opposed the law even before its passage, and the law's Democratic cosponsors all abandoned their support for NCLB before the end of Bush's first term in office. Although one could oppose NCLB on the grounds that its continued implementation would be bad for public education in 2004, the law could not reasonably be held responsible for the existing failures of the public schools. But by 2010, NCLB had been directing the federal effort to improve public education for more than eight years, making a discussion of its consequences more realistic. So when Diane Ravitch converted from an NCLB supporter to one of its harshest critics, she joined a chorus of parents, educators, scholars, politicians, and other public figures who blamed NCLB for the failures of public education during the 2000s. Ravitch's work has come to epitomize this new narrative, which blames NCLB's draconian application of high-stakes testing for narrowing public school curricula, misguidedly punishing struggling schools, and distorting the purpose of public education from the preparation for citizenship to the pursuit of test scores.

This new blame narrative is a departure from some thirty years of publicly blaming the schools themselves for educational failure. Even Kozol, who saw segregation as the overarching problem with public education in the United States, found the problems with segregation expressed at the level of the schools, drawing attention to the inequalities between them. However, for Ravitch and the millions of Americans who shared her disdain for NCLB, the problem was not the schools, but the federal law governing them.[12] Although the blaming of NCLB has shattered a political consensus about who should be held responsible when the public schools fail to live up to the nation's expectations, it has reinforced the rhetorical consensus that the public schools are in a state of failure and that education policy can only be advanced by finding the right place to pin public blame.

The Every Student Succeeds Act of 2015 (ESSA) is not the full expression of the still-evolving post-NCLB education politics. Whatever that new policy ultimately ends up being, it will need to respond to the concern that it not become the cause of educational failure by overtesting, narrowing the curriculum, or abandoning the citizen-making function of public education. In addition, it will do well not to push too far beyond Americans' traditional conception of what makes a school good or bad, lest the public become convinced that the laws, not the schools, have a distorted measure of educational achievement. For better and worse, these constraints guarantee that the new education policies that result from the emerging consensus will be homologous with the policies of the past, making change only after successfully redirecting public blame. Moreover, this continued reliance on public blame ensures that education policy will remain focused on the question of accountability, as those who are to blame must be held to account.[13] As long as policy changes are justified by blaming, the politics of education policy will revolve around the management of blame, with each stakeholder seeking to ensure that someone else is perceived as accountable. The result is not just the recycling of accountability-based reforms, but a dysfunctional public discourse of education policy.

PUBLIC BLAME AND THE FALL OF PUBLIC EDUCATION

Each instance of public blame in the deliberation over federal education policy advantages accountability-based reforms, even when blame is employed by advocates who oppose NCLB and other forms of accountability. However, as a trend, the excessive use of public blame also poses another problem for the deliberation over federal education policy: it sows the sort of mistrust and suspicion that forestalls discussion and compromise. Public education is a national enterprise. The public schools cannot and will not please all Americans, but they also will not function at their best without the support and participation of a broad majority of the American people. So, when the public discussion of education policy is dominated by relentless accusation, participation, discussion, and compromise become impossible and the politics of education disintegrates. Disparate interests lead in disparate directions and the idea that one system, however decentralized, can create an educational experience acceptable to all, or nearly all, Americans loses credibility.

Indeed, examples of disintegration abound. The public discussion of the Common Core State Standards Initiative is a case in point. A set of learning objectives adopted voluntarily by most of the states as well as the District of Columbia, Common Core became controversial when various political groups accused the consortium of invading students' privacy by sharing their testing data, teaching "offensive" books by authors like Toni Morrison, and mounting a federal and/or corporate power grab over public education. Although there were plenty of good reasons to oppose Common Core—like its complicity with accountability, propensity to narrow the curriculum, and doubts over whether it would improve achievement where NCLB had failed to—the public discussion of the initiative rarely reflected those concerns.[14] Indeed, the concerns that came to typify the deliberation over Common Core had little grounding in reality. In fact, Common Core required no new data collection. The initiative was, by definition, state-led, not a federal or corporate takeover.[15] In addition to those misconceptions, opposing the teaching of *The Bluest Eye* in public school classrooms is a telling synecdoche for the often fractious and anti-intellectual politics of those calling for the repeal of the Common Core.

Unfortunately, concerns over Common Core often took a conspiratorial tone on both the left and the right.[16] On the right, Governor Bobby Jindal of Louisiana insisted that Common Core was an example of the federal government "making curriculum decisions for our local classrooms." On the left, protesters accused the Common Core of being a corporate scheme to make money off of new curricular materials, a criticism applicable to almost every school reform effort in American history.[17] Either accusation would make more sense if the Common Core contained any curricular material, but it does not. The Common Core State Standards Initiative is what its title declares—a set of standards that each state pursues through whatever curriculum it chooses.

Confusion over the details of Common Core was so widespread that it spawned several efforts to set the record straight. For example, former Florida governor Jeb Bush and Indiana governor Mike Pence both created websites to help inform concerned citizens.[18] In addition, the Common Core Initiative itself put up a "Myths vs. Facts" section on its website that remained into 2016.[19] These attempts to correct popular misconceptions failed to save the initiative in the public mind, as many governors like Pence eventually caved, either repealing Common Core or joining the call for their state legislatures to repeal it.[20] More concerning than the fate of the Common Core, though, was the conspiratorial tone of those who opposed it. Painting Common Core as the product of a hidden federal or corporate agenda, its opposition resorted to improbable accusations in their effort to tie Common Core to familiar blame narratives. In a deliberative environment where conspiracy theories motivate political action, all evidence, especially inconvenient facts, is treated as more proof of the conspiracy.[21] Thus, it should be no surprise that reasoned appeals like fact checking failed to persuade Common Core's sternest opponents.

Not just a Common Core phenomenon, the paranoid style of education politics—through blaming—has created controversies and impacted policy on the state and local level. For example, in both Colorado and Oklahoma, conservative officeholders have attacked the Advanced Placement US history course on the grounds that it presents too negative a view of American history. In Jefferson County, Colorado, a sprawling suburban area west of Denver, a group of conservative school board members set up a committee to review the district's curricular materials, citing the AP tests as justification.[22] The board members were eventually voted out of office, but their organizational backers, Americans for Prosperity–Colorado, vowed to fight on.[23] In Oklahoma, despite public outcry, state-level representatives passed legislation ordering the state Board of Education to begin testing a replacement for the AP US history course on the ironic grounds that the AP course focused too much on the country's mistakes.[24] In both cases, the rhetorical strategy of blaming outsiders for tampering with the curriculum of the local schools jeopardized the availability of a course that is typically understood as evidence of a high-quality high school education. In addition, the use of blame to generate controversies focused on the content of the AP US history course reflects the difficulty of constructing any publicly acceptable curriculum when conflicting senses of America's history and identity are addressed through a discussion of education policy beset by divisive rhetoric.

The abuse of public blame is easy to find in the public speech of negligent politicians or misguided citizens, but the political exigencies it creates can entice academics to join in. For example, consider the Program on Education Policy and Governance (PEPG) located in Harvard University's Kennedy School of Government, funded in part by gifts from the Walton family of Walmart fame. The PEPG regularly publishes reports stressing the dire condition of America's schools based on the research of scholars who support various conservative educational causes, like school choice, accountability, and high-stakes testing.[25] Regardless of the merit of the PEPG's preferred policy solutions, their rhetoric relies on fear appeals and blame. Concluding their 2014 report, *Not Just a Problem for Other People's Children*, PEPG authors Eric A. Hanushek, Paul E. Peterson, and Ludger Woessmann insist that "there can be little doubt that educational shortcomings in the United States spread well beyond the corridors of the inner city or the confines of low-income neighborhoods." According to them, "the overall picture is distressing to those concerned about the well-being of the United States in the 21st century."[26]

More than just a touch of hyperbole in the conclusion of a report designed to promote PEPG research with the public, this language reflects the authors' desire to impress upon the American people the dire condition of their public education system as a deliberate rhetorical strategy. Later in the same conclusion they discuss their intentions:

> What remains to be done is to convince politically influential members of the well-educated segment of society that the problems are not isolated to other groups but can be found close to home. Without good information, it has been too easy for even sophisticated Americans to be seduced by apologists who would have the public believe the problems are simply those of poor kids in central-city schools. As long as the focus remains on distinctions within the United States, then the comfortable can remain comforted by the distance between suburbia and the inner city. But once the focus shifts to countries abroad and fair apples-to-apples comparisons are made, it becomes manifest that nearly all of our young people—from privileged and not-so-privileged backgrounds—are not faring well.[27]

For the PEPG, the problem with the politics of education is that middle-class Americans are not adequately frightened of their schools.

Moreover, "apologists" are to blame for preventing middle-class Americans from feeling scared enough to demand action. This is public blame endorsed as a rhetorical strategy for manipulating the deliberation over US education policy by a partnership between one of higher education's most generous donors and its most prestigious university. The prospects for a healthy deliberation over the future of the public education system, a deliberation that would ideally be based on research and reporting from trustworthy sources like specialized programs at premier universities, are substantially undercut when what should be the very best source of nonpartisan educational scholarship openly aspires to agitate instead of inform. Preferring the pursuit of politics over that of knowledge, the PEPG and academic entities like it abdicate their role as leaders in a policy-making process that should, even when it fails to improve public education, at least produce decisions defensible as the result of the best deliberation a democratic society can offer.[28]

Of course, academics on the right are not alone in embracing blame as a way to make their scholarship appealing to the public. Ravitch's most recent work, *Reign of Error: The Hoax of the Privatization Movement and the Danger to America's Public Schools*, discusses the education reforms of the era of accountability in often conspiratorial terms, accusing corporate America of scheming to infiltrate and subvert public education. This blame narrative is reflected in both the content and the form of Ravitch's current work. In her scholarship and advocacy, Ravitch has eloquently told the story of the transformation of education policy over the past thirty years. But also, by publishing two books, a high-profile blog, and a slew of op-eds, Ravitch has made an attempt to turn the tide of educational policy making back in favor of public education by wielding the same rhetorical tools that have gotten things so far off track, including a divisive brand of blame.

Altogether, the result of so much public blame is a deliberative context in which there is little incentive for pursuing the constitutive power of public deliberation, like community building and the discovery of common ground. The public discussion of education policy ought to reflect our best hopes for what the public schools should teach American children, modeling democratic skills like decorum and compromise in a way that appreciates the interests and humanity of all involved, even as individuals and groups lobby for opposing interests. Instead, the profusion of public blame in the deliberation of education policy encourages us to see the other side as irredeemable and ill-willed, preventing the building of trust, forestalling the pursuit of negotiation, and ultimately undermining the universal sense of investment that should make public education a collective effort to uplift all Americans.

AN END FOR THE DELIBERATION OF EDUCATION POLICY

The public deliberation President Carter initiated when he founded the Department of Education in 1979 has come to include a great deal of public blame. To be clear, though, this does not mean that the founding of ED or Carter's invitation for the public to discuss education as a national issue are in and of themselves bad things. Education did not become political in 1979; it always had been. Among many other things, education was at the center of desegregation, the most important social and political transformation of twentieth-century America. However, as the politics of education have come to resemble their contemporary electoral politics, education policy makers now must pursue public support amid a rhetorical milieu with more bifurcation and less nonpartisanship. As educational policy makers turn to public blame to persuade the American people to support their reforms, they often undermine our collective faith in the prospects of public education. This rhetorical environment favors reforms grounded in accountability, but it also favors reforms won by rejecting instead of embracing compromise. Ultimately, this kind of politics poses an existential threat to public education, because such dysfunctional political communication breeds doubt in our capacity as a nation to come together and responsibly manage important social institutions like schools.

In a larger sense, to whatever extent the US public schools system suffers the material consequences of the blame-ridden rhetoric we use to discuss it, public education has and will continue to suffer the rhetorical consequences of its degradation. Whether the public schools are or are not replaced by privately owned chartered equivalents or continue to educate the vast majority of American citizens, our system of education ceases to be meaningfully public when Americans stop believing in it as such. If we continue to undermine our public schools through the rhetoric of public blame, no one will regard them as our nation's premier institution enacting the educational will of the people, regardless of their earthly fate. Through our discussions of education policy, we express our best understanding of the current state of our schools and our best wishes for their future. The rhetoric of education determines *ipso facto,* not just how, but whether the American people value their public school system. In this sense, we all have decisions to make and a role to play in the future of our public schools whenever we discuss them. Toward this end for the deliberation of education policy, the next chapter will explore some of the rhetorical possibilities confronting us at those moments when we so often choose to blame.

7

The Paradox of Public Blame: A Future for US Education Policy

After creating the Department of Education (ED) in October 1979, one of President Jimmy Carter's first administrative tasks was to select the nation's first secretary of education. For the new job Carter tapped Shirley Hufstedler, an experienced federal appellate court judge he had been considering for a Supreme Court vacancy that never occurred during his presidency. As the inaugural US secretary of education, much of Hufstedler's time was spent introducing her new department to its various constituencies across the country. On Leap Day in 1980, Hufstedler was doing just that before a meeting of the Illinois Education Association in Chicago when she shared her thoughts about the politics of education:

> From the first day of our republic, the problems of American education have been the center of public controversy. National expectations of the schools in dealing with great social problems have always been high. These conditions are not now and never have been signs of weakness. Rather, they are evidence of a healthy national capacity for self-examination—constructive criticism, not cynicism—and of a deep and

> abiding faith in the strength of our educational system. They are, in short, the vital signs of success in a free and informed nation, a nation educated by design to handle the tumultuous style and the extreme demands of participatory democracy.
>
> In other words, the endless controversy that surrounds you as educators is, in many respects, your greatest achievement. How's that for irony? . . . Well, nobody ever said education was easy.[1]

For Hufstedler, the rough-and-tumble of the politics of education was among the "vital signs" of its "success." The "greatest achievement" of public education was affirmed in the "tumultuous style and the extreme demands of participatory democracy." According to the secretary, public education succeeds when democracy thrives, unbounded and unbridled. Because the politics of education are at "the center of public controversy," Hufstedler reasoned that they are at their best when they reflect the unrestrained condition of contemporary political discourse.

Hufstedler's posture toward the public deliberation over education policy found a silver lining in the rhetorical strife surrounding the establishment of the ED. It also projected magnanimity toward those who were saying that her new position should not exist. Moreover, the secretary was right; democracy loses its meaning if it fails to maintain space for disagreement. But, much more important than whether educators should count turbulent public discussions as a success or a failure, Hufstedler asserted a foundational role for education in the making of American politics. According to Hufstedler, deliberations over education policy are not microcosmic reflections of American politics broadly construed; they are constitutive of it. I could not agree more. In addition to its other functions, public education has a responsibility to foster public discourse, a process that inevitably turns back upon education and makes it the subject of the discourse it gave rise to. Moreover, debates over education policy should not reflect the kind of public deliberation that typifies American politics; they should set the example for the kind of discourse that *ought* to typify American politics. However, this requires reckoning the role of public blame in the rhetoric of education policy.

BETTER BLAME MAKES FOR BETTER EDUCATION POLICY

Political rhetoric is equipment for policy making, and as a result, the health of our political speech is inevitably reflected in the health of our public policy.[2] As political rhetoric, blame is paradoxical. It relies on a generally held belief in the persuasive power of deliberation, but as a means of discursive belligerence, a profusion of blaming can undermine the same faith in deliberation it depends upon. The past three decades of educational politics have been overcrowded with blame, transforming it into a corrupting and destructive force. Nonetheless, this does not mean that we should aspire to a public discussion devoid of blame. Rhetorically bloodless deliberation would be facile. When blame brings important issues to the public's attention, puncturing a consensus that is held together by apathy or ignorance, it invigorates our civic culture. As a consequence, any effort to improve the public discussion of education policy must encourage helpful forms of blame as well as discourage unhelpful ones, all while weighing the ill effects of unscrupulous speech against the ill effects of regulating speech. But if we are to improve the public discussion of education policy by cultivating better public blame, how can we parse helpful and harmful kinds of blame? And, how might such parsing help guide us toward a better rhetoric of education policy and, ultimately, toward better education policy itself?

Blame is an important and necessary mode of political speech. Just like any other rhetorical device, blame should be used in a way that upholds the values of a democratic society. Understanding it as such, the distinction between harmful and helpful blame is not nearly as difficult to make as it is to practice. Nonetheless, several distinguishing characteristics bear discussing.

Frequency

Blame is an extreme rhetorical tactic. It almost always creates a rupture in a democratic community because it identifies a problem in urgent need of remedy, and that remedy usually involves some individual or group holding another individual or group accountable. For example, in "What's Wrong with Our Schools?" Milton Friedman blamed bureaucrats for ruining public education both in the abstract, during a newsmagazine-style report, and in person, during a face-to-face debate. Friedman's indirect belligerence toward bureaucrats as a group began an argument that had its logical end in his direct belligerence toward the educational experts who joined him for the debate. In this way, Friedman modeled the sort of thought and action he advocated for parents, whom he encouraged to take decision-making power away from bureaucrats. Taken seriously, blame is a big deal for any society that makes its most consequential decisions via deliberation. However, when blame is overused, it loses its urgency and seriousness. It becomes blasé. When every other advocate calls for an overthrow of the bureaucracy like Friedman, fewer of them are likely to be taken seriously. Worse still, when a normally sobering rhetorical tactic is misused, it undermines the value of deliberation. Blame should be used sparingly. Blaming less frequently would preserve the consequential nature of public deliberation as well as the persuasiveness of the policy advocates who, on occasion, must resort to it.

In addition, public blame is a cynical rhetorical tactic that can enculturate despair. Accusations appeal to our doubts and confirm our suspicions. It is easy to believe that a faceless collection of bureaucrats or a greedy cabal of corporate elites might have conspired to damage our schools. And, although it may be true that at times in our history that they have, the frequent repetition of a believable blame narrative can affix certain assumptions in the public mind. Unfortunately, those assumptions may have little to do with bureaucrats or CEOs or even the motives of the advocates who make cheap use of blame. For example, the near constant abuse of public blame to forward education policy since the founding of the ED has helped convince many Americans that the public schools are in a state of abject failure, a belief advantageous for far fewer of education policy's advocates than those who enthusiastically cast blame at their nearest foes. When blame is used over and over again, the cynicism it invokes becomes a habit, and citizens are conditioned to doubt all, even the best, plans for improving education. Blaming alone cannot create better education policy.

Proportionality

To reiterate, blame is a relatively extreme rhetorical tactic. In addition to using blame less frequently, public deliberation benefits when its participants take care to use blame proportionately. One difficulty in the public discussion of education policy has been the tendency of advocates to use blame to paint with an overly broad brush. Advocate after advocate proclaims that he, she, or they have found the cause of all public education's failures. For the National Commission on Excellence in Education (NCEE), a flagging commitment to educational excellence as evidenced by changes in SAT scores was responsible for imperiling the future prosperity and security of the entire nation. According to the NCLB, the street-level bureaucrats of education were solely responsible for any measurable losses in achievement. Although effective as policy advocacy, these blame narratives are reductive. They rely on unprovable oversimplifications and, as such, they fail either to model rigorous deliberation or to help create a better-informed public.

A proportionate use of blame would incorporate a clear explanation of how a particular cause and effect are related and, in most cases, would need to avoid making reductive claims about the cause's vast effects—like nationwide changes in educational achievement—with a great number of potential explanations. After all, "educational achievement" can be defined in any number of ways. Even supplanting the discussion of achievement with more specific outcomes like test scores, dropout rates, rates of college admission, or grade-level promotion would be more honest. However, the same rule must be applied for discussions of issues like inequality. Using more modest blame narratives that connect specific decisions to specific outcomes would result in a rhetorical exchange where competing claims could be meaningfully compared. This kind of specificity exists in education research and scholarship, but as it stands, the public discussion of education by policy advocates interested in persuading the public often lacks specificity and clarity, most especially when advocates turn to blame.

Unifying Versus Dividing

Most blame is divisive; it puts responsibility on an individual or group while calling others to hold that individual or group responsible. When Friedman blamed educational bureaucrats, he divided them from parents, even though the two should ideally work together for the benefit of each child. When Diane Ravitch blamed NCLB and the coalition of corporate and politically conservative interests that helped create the law for damaging America's schools during the 2000s, she sought the support of parents as well as politically liberal interests to defeat the law she had once supported. That said, public blame can also be a tool for unification. By blaming itself as well as the entire nation for the failures of public education, the NCEE used public blame to bring the nation together. According to *A Nation at Risk*, all Americans had a responsibility for maintaining and pursuing high academic standards. Similarly, in *Savage Inequalities*, Jonathan Kozol insisted that Americans in general had a responsibility to aid in the effort to desegregate schools.

From time to time, blame—assuming it is infrequent and proportionate—might need to be used in a divisive way to achieve a much-needed policy change that will never have anything close to unanimous support. Policy advocates should not feel obligated to make their arguments more appealing to racists, for example. Some political views should be left out on ethical grounds. However, policy advocates should ask themselves whether a unifying appeal might be more appropriate than one that divides, even when they are set on blaming. Public blame does not necessarily have to pit one group against another. Like any other rhetorical appeal, the constraints on public blame emerge from its audience. In the case of public blame, an advocate encourages that audience to join him or her in placing blame, but does not necessarily have to choose another group to blame. This is an especially important consideration for those who seek to reform public education in order to preserve it as a public enterprise. By blaming both themselves and their audience, the authors of *A Nation at Risk* created a unifying rhetorical appeal that most scholars now credit with setting the terms of the education policy debate for the following three decades. *A Nation at Risk* also helped to save the ED from President Reagan's threat to relegate it to an office. And in addition to its political effectiveness, the report popularized a vision of public education as crucial for the economic security of the nation. Overall, the NCEE's use of blame served to unify the nation and strengthen its commitment to education as a necessarily collective enterprise. Importantly, this larger war of position over the publicness of education is played out each time a policy advocate chooses to use blame to unify or divide the nation in support of a new policy.

Public Welfare Versus Political Strategy

In addition to considering whether to use blame to unify or divide, policy advocates would do well to consider the degree to which a particular act of blame promises to benefit the public welfare versus benefiting their political strategy. This is not to say that advocates must know the unknowable—whether their preferred policy reform will in fact improve the fate of the public schools in the way they promise—but that their advocacy must be an act of commitment to the public welfare more than an act of political gamesmanship. Once again, when blame appears to pursue political advantage to the exclusion of the public welfare, it can undermine the civic faith it relies on to be effective as a rhetorical strategy.

The potential imbalance between her appeal to the public welfare and her attempt to successfully pursue a political position is the danger that impelled Ravitch to narrate her conversion in *The Death and Life of the Great American School System*. Without giving an account of how and why she had come to believe that NCLB had hurt American education during the 2000s, Ravitch's act of public blame against NCLB might have been presumed a crass political maneuver. To an extent, this required Ravtich to risk her reputation as a public figure by admitting that she had been wrong about many of the reforms built into NCLB. Discrediting more than a decade of her own past policy advocacy, Ravitch's act of public blaming displayed a willingness to put the public welfare ahead of political gain. Ravitch's risk taking helped ensure the success of her advocacy, but it also modeled the kind of public blame that has the potential to enrich public discussion—at least in the case of *The Death and Life of the Great American School System*. To avoid undermining the power of public deliberation, advocates who use blame must convincingly justify their rhetoric as a pursuit of the public welfare despite the fact that such civic verisimilitude often comes at great political risk. Whether such advocacy is accepted at face value or rejected as a rhetorical double-cross, it still reinforces the socially held value that the public discussion of education policy should put ethics and honesty above political gain because it seeks legitimacy on those grounds.

PRAISE FOR THE POLITICS OF EDUCATION

So far, all of these suggestions have the potential to improve the quality of public blaming. But if blame risks undermining the civic faith necessary for democratic deliberation as well as creating sufficient acrimony to lead Americans to doubt their ability to collectively manage education as a public enterprise, why use it at all? Certainly blame can be a positive force in deliberation, but there is an entire world of argumentative strategies. If education policy advocates really should blame less, what should they do instead? There must be some alternative strategy capable of creating effective advocacy without simultaneously risking such a catastrophic outcome for public education. Indeed, there are many rhetorical devices that might constitute an improvement over either the continued abuse of blame or even the responsible use of blame, but the careful consideration of how and why would require a book on the ins and outs of each alternative device. Nonetheless, within the scope of this book, one particular strategy stands out for consideration. Blame is not an only child. Blame has a rhetorical twin—its opposite—in praise. Together praise (*epainos*) and blame (*psogos*) form the two halves of what Aristotle called ceremonial (*epideictic*) speech. Since many of the dynamics that apply to blame also apply, albeit in the opposite way, to praise, its merits can be efficiently considered here.

In much the same way that blame can be used to identify the roots of an educational failure, praise can be used to call attention to educational success. This can be as simple as identifying the key characteristics of a successful school or pointing to a district that has undergone a reform that resulted in the desired improvement. "When you want to set out proposals in deliberation," advised Aristotle, "see what you would praise."[3] Through examples of triumph as opposed to tragedy, praise can shape deliberation and make one's advocacy vibrant without simultaneously promoting cynicism. This does not mean that praise is guaranteed to be accurate; some apparent successes can turn out to be fleeting or even the product of deception. Additionally, an advocate must select how to praise with the same care he or she would give to selecting who or what to blame. For example, an advocate can choose whether to use praise in relation to specific accomplishments or the successful embodiment of virtues. According to Aristotle: "Praise [*epainos*] is speech that makes clear the virtue [of the subject praised]," whereas "*encomium*, in contrast, is concerned with deeds."[4] Praising the embodiment of virtues is one way to avoid saddling oneself to deeds that may prove iniquitous. In addition to avoiding the promotion of cynicism, regularly featuring successes in the public deliberation of education policy might actually improve the nation's confidence in its public school system. If an education policy advocate aims to create change without also creating a deliberation that undercuts the publicness of schooling, he or she should at least consider using praise before resolving to blame, especially given that they both call audiences to transform their convictions into action.

Like blame, praise is not new to the public discussion of education policy, but also like blame, it comes in many forms. For example, when George H. W. Bush publicly acknowledged Kozol's scathing observations from *Savage Inequalities*, he did so at an event honoring the nation's best schools, juxtaposing their successes with the failures Kozol chronicled. The National Blue Ribbon Schools Program, created by Secretary of Education Terrel Bell during Ronald Reagan's first term in office, recognizes the accomplishments of the country's best and most-improved public and private schools each year.[5] However, the program praises in a ceremonial context; it is not an example of the use of praise as an overtly deliberative strategy.

By contrast, George W. Bush's remarks at the Boston Latin School on the day he signed NCLB into law offer an example of deliberative praise in public discussion of education policy:

> . . . if you look at this bill that I signed this morning in Ohio, it says this is the way—this is Boston Latin all over again. This is what Boston Latin is about. It's about expecting high standards, understanding every child can learn, demanding the best, insisting upon hard work, rewarding success, solving failure. It is a great school, and I am grateful that I could come and herald the signing of an important piece of legislation here at this school. This is not only a testimony to Senator Ted Kennedy's hard work; it's a testimony to a fine public school.[6]

Here, at the height of the bipartisanship immediately following September 11, Ted Kennedy's high school alma mater served as an exemplar. According to President Bush, Boston Latin embodied the highest educational virtues: "high standards, understanding every child can learn, demanding the best, insisting upon hard work, rewarding success, solving failure." Praising Athenians in Athens, Bush's compliments earned him goodwill that he then attempted to transfer to NCLB.[7] Statements like this one helped make NCLB a popular, bipartisan law when it was initially passed. Whether Bush's transfer device succeeded or failed in this particular moment, it nevertheless expressed great confidence in a notable public school.[8] By praising a successful school, Bush prepared his audience to see a better future in the emerging educational status quo under NCLB, but he also affirmed the potential for schooling to succeed as a public enterprise. According to Bush, every school could be a Boston Latin.

Certainly, praise has its own potential hazards. Barack Obama's much maligned Race to the Top Fund, passed as part of the American Recovery and Reinvestment Act of 2009, set aside billions in federal grants and then awarded them on a competitive basis to eighteen of the states and the District of Columbia. Designed to reward states who "trail-blaze effective reforms and provide examples for States and local school districts throughout the country to follow," Race to the Top pursued many of the same policy goals as NCLB—school choice and accountability—but attempted to motivate their pursuit with a formal process of praise, rather than blame.[9] Implemented alongside NCLB, Race to the Top encountered many difficulties. Among other things, it was criticized for launching a federal takeover of education policy, duplicating and/or supporting the implementation of NCLB, unfairly rewarding already advantaged states, and engaging in political favoritism.[10] However laudable the fund's goals may have been, Race to the Top's public relations difficulties highlight the rhetorical pitfalls of public praise. Having failed to win support from the program after the first of three rounds of funding, some states chose not to reapply. Unlike public blame, where rejection of the accusation is an expected part of the exchange that bears very little on the legitimacy of the act, public praise can be undermined when it is disavowed by those who are supposed to seek it. Praise must be valued by both actual and potential recipients or it fails to inspire change. The refusal of some states to participate in the Race to the Top competition cast doubt on the Obama administration's characterization of the winning states as trail-blazing leaders.

Altogether, public praise offers a compelling alternative to public blame, especially for policy advocates who hope to push policy without intentionally evoking cynicism. Although the Race to the Top example demonstrates that cynicism can develop as a response, praise itself is simply much less likely to undermine the publicness of education. However, commending educators and educational institutions for exemplifying the best virtues of education as opposed to lauding specific accomplishments will help advocates give their praises more defensibly. But what can those who are not directly engaged in crafting communicative appeals for education reform contribute to the rhetoric of education policy?

AN INTERPRETIVE TRADITION FOR THE POLITICS OF EDUCATION

To this point, this chapter has given a great deal of guidance to aspirant policy makers. Hopefully, any present or future leaders who have read this far have appreciated all of the advice directed at them. But, since such public figures and power brokers are a relatively small slice of the public, most readers of this book—researchers, principals, teachers, parents, students, and the average citizen—probably still wonder what they can do about the abuse of public blame in the rhetoric of education policy. Unfortunately, when every advocate is enamored with blaming, shifting support from one reformer to another is no help. So, what would be a practical response for a frustrated follower of educational politics?

Often, the thoughtful discussion of the politics of education is at its best when it conceptualizes the struggle to achieve policy reform as a phenomenon that exists both within its particular context and as one moment in a history of many shifting contexts. In other words, each instantiation of the rhetoric of education policy exists in its time and as part of the history that informs other times. When we write and speak about education policy, we are forced to retell and thereby reinterpret its history. Often, blame creeps into the conversation through these retellings. The path we must choose to pursue a better future begins by sorting out our disappointment with the past, which is why the retelling of our educational history is so central to reform advocacy and why it needs our careful attention. Over time and regardless of intention, this continual process of interpretation and reinterpretation forms a tradition in which events like the publication of *A Nation at Risk* or the passage of the Elementary and Secondary Education Act of 1965 take on certain meanings, which are then contested. This is the interpretive tradition of education policy.

The study and the popular discussion of education policy do not want for controversy over the interpretation of the educational past. However, only rarely is the process of interpretation and the various forms it can take given much consideration. Led by the close reading of impactful and controversial texts from education policy's past, researchers and citizens together need to take hold of education policy's drifting interpretive tradition.[11] This would require asking critical questions about the connections between habits of interpretation and the shape of educational politics, such as: What are the consequences when reformers deploy a Whig history of US education in their advocacy? What are the prospects of political action grounded in poststructuralist accounts of political conflict over education?[12] Whom do we sanction to speak with authority about the nature of public education and how? This effort would require not only more rhetorical analyses of education policy texts by experts, but also the democratization of interpretive methods that would allow citizens and students to participate in managing the interpretation of America's educational past.[13] At the very least, the basic recognition of rhetorical commonplaces, such as recurring patterns of argument and other strategies for using persuasion to achieve policy change, and the consequences of accepting or contesting those arguments and strategies, would empower Americans to help direct the future rhetoric of education policy as opposed to merely being directed by it.

In the spirit of democratizing the interpretive tradition of education policy, the next time you hear a policy advocate resort to blame in an attempt to persuade you or those around you, consider these questions:

1. What constitutes educational success and failure for this advocate and what does not?

2. Which aspects of America's educational past has this advocate chosen to highlight and which has he or she chosen not to mention?
3. What role should the accused party ideally play in the improvement of public education according to this advocate and how is this act of blaming designed to encourage them to do so?
4. What does this act of blame contribute to the vibrancy and quality of the public discussion over education policy in proportion to the cynicism and division it evokes?
5. Would you be pleased if your fellow citizens discussed their public schools in the same way this advocate has at, for example, a school board meeting?

GRADUATING FROM ENDLESS BLAME

Blame would not find such fertile ground in the discussion of public education in the United States if Americans did not care so deeply about their schools and what they represent. Each of the endless accusations that the public schools are failing at their core mission of educating the next generation reinforces the importance of education, but the accumulated warning also invites Americans to doubt the capacity of public schools to ever live up to the expectations put upon them. Yet, whatever the success or failure the public schools achieve as a system, Americans will always need a healthy and productive political discourse concerning them in order to have any chance at achieving a better educational future. It is profoundly unlikely that good public policy will be made through a political process defined by cycles of manic reform and depressive panic.[14] Reconsidering the outsized role of blame in the public discussion of education policy, even if such a reconsideration were to result in a sweeping revolution in the rhetorical habits of American citizens and their political leaders, will not directly improve the schools. However, it would remove one particularly pernicious barrier depressing the collective effort to do so. Perhaps more importantly, such a reconsideration would require that Americans be more thoughtful about how they discuss education as a public enterprise. After all, giving greater care to the way we talk about our schools when we consider making sweeping changes to them may be the least blameworthy thing we can do.

Notes

Introduction

1. The first department of education was organized in 1865 under President Andrew Johnson. The department was demoted to an office in 1867. Lee W. Anderson, *Congress in the Classroom: From the Cold War to "No Child Left Behind"* (University Park: The Pennsylvania State University Press, 2007), 102, 129.
2. Jimmy Carter, "Department of Education Organization Act: Statement on Signing S. 210 into Law, October 17, 1979," *Public Papers of the President of the United States, 1979*, vol. 2 (Washington, DC: GPO, 1980), 1959.
3. Jimmy Carter, "Department of Education Organization Act: Remarks at the Bill Signing Ceremony, October 17, 1979," *Public Papers of the President of the United States, 1979*, vol. 2 (Washington, DC: GPO, 1980), 1955.
4. Carter, "Department of Education Organization Act: Statement," 1958.
5. Ibid., 1959.
6. Anderson, *Congress in the Classroom*, 127; see also Paul Manna, *School's In: Federalism and the National Education Agenda* (Washington, DC: Georgetown University Press, 2006), 66.
7. In the order that their preferred terms appear: Patricia Albjerg Graham, *Schooling America: How the Public Schools Meet the Nation's Changing Needs* (New York: Oxford University Press, 2005); David F. Labaree, *Someone Has to Fail: The Zero-Sum Game of Public Schooling* (Cambridge: Harvard University Press, 2010); Jal Mehta, *The Allure of Order: High Hopes, Dashed Expectations, and the Troubled Quest to Remake American Schooling* (New York: Oxford University Press, 2013).
8. Christopher Lubienski and Sarah Theule Lubienski, *The Public School Advantage: Why Public Schools Outperform Private Schools* (Chicago: University of Chicago Press, 2014), 3–6; Nel Noddings, *Education and Democracy in the 21st Century* (New York: Teachers College Press, 2013), 1–2.

9. "Achievement era" is Patrician Albjerg Graham's term for the present period of education reform stretching back to *A Nation at Risk*. Graham, *Schooling America*, 2.
10. Now the Omohundro Institute of Early American History and Culture. Attendees included Richard Hofstadter, Robert K. Merton, and Arthur Schlesinger. Lawrence Cremin later oversaw the resulting book's reprinting. Bernard Bailyn, *Education in the Forming of American Society: Needs and Opportunities for Study* (Chapel Hill: University of North Carolina Press, 1960), 48.
11. A list of the significant contributions to this contemporary conversation: Dana Goldstein, *Teacher Wars: A History of America's Most Embattled Profession* (New York: Doubleday, 2014); Graham, *Schooling America*; Jennifer L. Hochschild and Nathan B. Scovronick, *The American Dream and the Public Schools* (New York: Oxford University Press, 2003); Labaree, *Someone Has to Fail*; Meira Levinson, *No Citizen Left Behind* (Cambridge: Harvard University Press, 2012); Lubienski and Lubienski, *The Public School Advantage*; Mehta, *The Allure of Order*; William J. Reese, *Testing Wars in the Public Schools: A Forgotten History* (Cambridge: Harvard University Press, 2013); Jesse H. Rhodes, *An Education in Politics: The Origins and Evolution of No Child Left Behind* (Ithaca: Cornell University Press, 2012); Tracy Lynn Steffes, *School, Society, and State: A New Education to Govern Modern America, 1890–1940* (Chicago: University of Chicago Press, 2012). Many of these works owe a great deal to David Tyack and Larry Cuban's *Tinkering Toward Utopia: A Century of Public School Reform* (Cambridge: Harvard University Press, 1995).
12. Giandomenico Majone, *Evidence, Argument, and Persuasion in the Policy Process* (New Haven: Yale University Press, 1989), 1–11, 17, 19. Deborah Stone articulates a similar idea in her description of political reasoning: Deborah Stone, *Policy Paradox: The Art of Political Decision Making*, rev. ed. (New York: Norton, 2002), 381–83.
13. Aristotle, *On Rhetoric: A Theory of Civic Discourse*, trans. George A. Kennedy (New York: Oxford University Press, 2007), 37.
14. For more on the rhetoric of education policy: Linda Adler-Kassner and Susanmarie Harrington, "Responsibility and Composition's Future in the Twenty-First Century: Reframing 'Accountability,'" *College Composition and Communication* 62 (2010): 73–99; Robert Asen, "Lyndon Baines Johnson and George W. Bush on Education Reform: Ascribing Agency and Responsibility Through Key Policy Terms," *Rhetoric & Public Affairs* 15 (2012): 298–317; Robert Asen, *Democracy, Deliberation, and Education* (University Park: The Pennsylvania State University Press, 2015); Shawn Batt, "Keeping Company in Controversy: Education Reform, Spheres of Argument, and Ethical Criticism," *Argumentation and Advocacy* 40 (2003): 85–104; Louis M. Eich, "Charles W. Elliot," in *A History and Criticism of American Public Address*, vol. 2, ed. William Norwood Brigance (New York: Russell & Russell, 1960), 526–39; Charles A. Fritz, "Edwin A. Alderman," in *A History and Criticism of American Public Address*, vol. 2, ed. William Norwood Brigance (New York: Russell & Russell, 1960), 540–56; Stephanie Houston Grey, "The Statistical War on Equality: Visions of American Virtuosity in the Bell Curve," *Quarterly Journal of Speech* 85 (1999): 303–29; Robin E. Jensen, *Dirty Words: The Rhetoric of Public Sex Education, 1870–1924* (Champaign:

University of Illinois Press, 2010); Paige M. Hermansen, "'There Was No One Coming with Enough Power to Save Us': Waiting for 'Superman' and the Rhetoric of the New Education Documentary," *Rhetoric & Public Affairs* 17 (2014): 511–40; Mark Hlavacik, "The Democratic Origins of Teachers' Union Rhetoric: Margaret Haley's Speech at the 1904 NEA Convention," *Rhetoric & Public Affairs* 15 (2012): 499–524; Rebecca A. Kuehl, "The Rhetorical Presidency and 'Accountability' in Education Reform: Comparing the Presidential Rhetoric of Ronald Reagan and George W. Bush," *Southern Communication Journal* 77 (2012): 329–48; Kristen Olsen Lanier, "'Harken to the Sound of the Trumpet': 'A Nation at Risk' as an American Jeremiad" (presentation, Annual Meeting of the American Education Research Association, New Orleans, LA, 2000): 1–19; Mark Garrett Longaker, *Rhetoric and the Republic: Politics, Civic Discourse, and Education in Early America* (Tuscaloosa: University of Alabama Press, 2007); Holly G. McIntush, "Defining Education: The Rhetorical Enactment of Ideology in A Nation at Risk," *Rhetoric & Public Affairs* 3 (2000): 419–43; Holly G. McIntush, "Political Truancy: George Bush's Claim to the Mantle 'Education President,'" in *The Rhetorical Presidency of George H. W. Bush*, ed. Martin J. Medhurst (College Station: Texas A&M University Press, 2006), 102–18; Kendall R. Phillips, *Testing Controversy: A Rhetoric of Educational Reform* (Cresskill, NJ: Hampton Press, 2004); Ann Q. Staton and Jennifer A. Peeples, "Educational Reform Discourse: President George Bush on 'America 2000,'" *Communication Education* 49 (2000): 303–9; Michael J. Steudeman, "'The Guardian Genius of Democracy": The Myth of the Heroic Teacher in Lyndon B. Johnson's Education Policy Rhetoric, 1964–1966," *Rhetoric & Public Affairs* 17 (2014): 477–510; Michael J. Steudeman, "Indeterminacy, Incipiency, and Attitudes: Materialist Oscillation in the 2012 Chicago Teachers' Strike," *Quarterly Journal of Speech* 101 (2015): 509–33; Karen Tracy, *Challenges of Ordinary Democracy: A Case Study in Deliberation and Dissent* (University Park: The Pennsylvania State University Press, 2010).

15. Larry Cuban, "Reforming Again, Again, and Again," *Educational Researcher* 19 (1990): 3–13.
16. Even with the passage of the Every Student Succeeds Act of 2016 to replace NCLB, accountability remains the key watchword of education policy: Dana Mitra, "No Child Left Behind's Replacement Isn't Much of a Replacement," *Penn Live*, January 27, 2016, http://www.pennlive.com/opinion/2016/01/no_child_left_behinds_replacem.html; Alia Wong, "The Bloated Rhetoric of No Child Left Behind's Demise," *The Atlantic*, December 9, 2015, http://www.theatlantic.com/education/archive/2015/12/the-bloated-rhetoric-of-no-child-left-behinds-demise/419688/.
17. Larry Cuban, *Hugging the Middle: How Teachers Teach in an Era of Testing and Accountability* (New York: Teachers College Press, 2009), 14.
18. David Zarefsky, "Four Senses of Rhetorical History," in *Doing Rhetorical History: Concepts and Cases*, ed. Kathleen Turner (Tuscaloosa: University of Alabama Press, 2003), 19–32.
19. P. F. Strawson, *Freedom and Resentment and Other Essays* (1974; repr., New York: Routledge, 2008), 1–28. For additional reading: Brynmor Browne, "A Solution to the Problem of Moral Luck," *Philosophical Quarterly* 42 (1992): 343–56; Nan Goodman,

Shifting the Blame: Literature, Law, and the Theory of Accidents in Nineteenth-Century America (Princeton: Princeton University Press, 1998); Christopher Hood, *The Blame Game: Spin, Bureaucracy, and Self-Preservation in Government* (Princeton: University of Princeton Press, 2011); Sharon Lamb, *The Trouble with Blame: Victims, Perpetrators, and Responsibility* (Cambridge: Harvard University Press, 1996); Thomas Nagel, "Moral Luck," in *Moral Luck*, ed. Daniel Statman (Albany: State University of New York Press, 1993), 57–72; George Sher, *In Praise of Blame* (New York: Oxford University Press, 2006); Charles Tilly, *Credit and Blame* (Princeton: Princeton University Press, 2008); Bernard Williams, "Moral Luck," in *Moral Luck*, ed. Daniel Statman (Albany: State University of New York Press, 1993), 35–56.

20. Tyack and Cuban, *Tinkering Toward Utopia*, 14.
21. Aristotle, *On Rhetoric*, 75–83.
22. Kenneth Burke, *A Grammar of Motives* (Berkeley: University of California Press, 1969), 406–8; Kenneth Burke, "The Rhetoric of Hitler's Battle," in *The Philosophy of Literary Form* (Berkeley: University of California Press, 1973), 191–221.
23. Michael Warner, *Publics and Counterpublics* (New York: Zone Books, 2005).
24. Goodman, *Shifting the Blame*; Jules Holroyd, "A Communicative Concept of Moral Appraisal," *Ethical Theory and Moral Practice* 10 (2007): 267–78; Nagel, "Moral Luck"; Lamb, *The Trouble with Blame*; Sher, *In Praise of Blame*; Richard Sorabji, *Necessity, Cause, and Blame: Perspectives on Aristotle's Theory* (Ithaca: Cornell University Press, 1980); Allen Speight, "'Listening to Reason': The Role of Persuasion in Aristotle's Account of Praise, Blame, and the Voluntary," *Philosophy & Rhetoric* 38 (2005): 213–25; J. E. R. Squires, "Blame," *Philosophical Quarterly* 18 (1968): 54–60; Lawrence Stern, "Freedom, Blame, and Moral Community," *The Journal of Philosophy* 71 (1974): 72–84; Tilly, *Credit and Blame*; Williams, "Moral Luck"; Browne, "A Solution to the Problem of Moral Luck"; Garrath Williams, "Blame and Moral Responsibility," *Ethical Theory and Moral Practice* 6 (2003): 427–45.
25. For a discussion of how speakers construct their audiences, see Chaim Perelman and L. Olbrechts-Tyteca, *The New Rhetoric: A Treatise on Argumentation* (Notre Dame: University of Notre Dame Press, 1969), 19–21. Public blaming in the American protestant tradition comes in the form of sermons called jeremiads. Unlike the sort of blame I am investigating here, these acts of blame are designed to motivate the group that is being blamed. For additional reading: Sacvan Bercovitch, *The American Jeremiad* (Madison: University of Wisconsin Press, 1978); David Howard-Pitney, *The African American Jeremiad: Appeals for Justice in America* (Philadelphia: Temple University Press, 2005).
26. In this way, public blame is a speech act. Austin, for example, considered it briefly under the term *accusation*. J. L. Austin, *How to Do Things with Words* (Cambridge: Harvard University Press, 1962); John R. Searle, *Speech Acts: An Essay in the Philosophy of Language* (London: Cambridge University Press, 1969).
27. Edward Schiappa, *The Beginnings of Rhetorical Theory in Classical Greece* (New Haven: Yale University Press, 1999).

28. For more on the sophists, see John Poulakos, *Sophistical Rhetoric in Ancient Greece* (Columbia: University of South Carolina Press, 1995).
29. In order, I am alluding to: Rhodes, *An Education in Politics*, 8–10; Labaree, *Someone Has to Fail*, 10–41; Graham, *Schooling America*, 153–61; Mehta, *The Allure of Order*, 17–23.
30. Mehta, *The Allure of Order*, 214–17.
31. Raquel Farmer-Hinton, Joi D. Lewis, Lori D. Patton, and Ishwanzya D. Rivers, "Dear Mr. Kozol. . . . Four African American Women Scholars and the Re-Authoring of Savage Inequalities," *Teachers College Record* 115 (2013): 1–38.
32. Jeffrey R. Henig, *The End of Exceptionalism in American Education: The Changing Politics of School Reform* (Cambridge, MA: Harvard Education Press, 2013); Labaree, *Someone Has to Fail*, 2012. Kenneth A. Sirotnik, ed., *Holding Accountability Accountable: What Ought to Matter in Public Education* (New York: Teachers College Press, 2004).

Chapter 1

1. Milton Friedman, "What's Wrong with Our Schools?," *Free to Choose*, episode 6 (Erie, PA: Free to Choose Enterprise, 1980), DVD.
2. Friedman's neoliberalism, in the case of "What's Wrong with Our Schools?," is his insistence that education would be managed better by a market than the state. Suzy Harris, *The Governance of Education: How Neo-Liberalism Is Transforming Policy and Practice* (London: Continuum, 2007), 20–21.
3. John Kenneth Galbraith, *The Age of Uncertainty* (Boston: Houghton Mifflin, 1977). The television series was directed by Mick Jackson and is easiest to obtain on YouTube.
4. Friedman first made his case in print in 1955. He later represented his argument in a more popular forum, his own book *Capitalism and Freedom*. The essays from both publications are almost identical save some changes in phrasing and examples. Friedman points out the few substantive changes himself in footnotes in *Capitalism and Freedom*. Milton Friedman, "The Role of Government in Education," in *Economics and the Public Interest: Essays Written in Honor of Eugene Ewald Agger*, ed. Robert A. Solo (New Brunswick, NJ: Rutgers University Press, 1955), 123–43; Milton Friedman, *Capitalism and Freedom* (Chicago: University of Chicago Press, 1962), 85–107.
5. Jeffrey R. Henig, *Rethinking School Choice: Limits of the Market Metaphor* (Princeton: Princeton University Press, 1994), 6.
6. I use *logical fallacy* to describe *ad hominem* because that is the most recognizable term for it that I know. Of course, Aristotle considered these abuses of *logos*, not logic. Contemporary philosophers and pragma-dialecticians often use the term *informal logic* to refer to the analysis of arguments out in the world. I prefer *rhetoric* for that, but in the case of *ad hominem*, I think *logical fallacy* communicates best. Aristotle, *On Sophistical Refutations*, trans. E. S. Foster, Loeb Classical Library (Cambridge, MA: Harvard University Press, 1955).
7. The most sophisticated understanding and study of the *ad hominem* as a rhetorical tactic in action has been accomplished by a group of Dutch scholars who approach

rhetoric as "pragma-dialectics." For the pragma-dialecticians, argumentation theory, which they cull from both the rhetorical and philosophical traditions in the West, is the grounds for the empirical study of argumentative discourse as it unfolds. For some of their work on the *ad hominem*, see Gabriel Nuchelmans, "On the Fourfold Root of the Argumentum Ad Hominem," in *Empirical Logic and Public Debate: Essays in Honour of Else M. Barth*, eds. Erik C. W. Krabbe, Renee Jose Dalitz, and Pier A. Smit (Amsterdam: Radopi, 1993), 37–47; D. N. Walton, "Search for the Roots of the Circumstantial *Ad Hominem*," *Argumentation* 15 (2001): 207–21; Frans van Eemeren, Bart Garssen, and Bert Meuffels, *Fallacies and Judgments of Reasonableness: Empirical Research Concerning the Pragma-Dialectical Rules* (New York: Springer, 2009), 6–8, 51–56.

8. Henry W. Johnstone, "Locke and Whately on *Argumentum Ad Hominem*," *Argumentation* 10 (1996): 89–97.
9. Katarzyna Budzynska and Maciej Witek, "Non-Inferential Aspects of *Ad Hominem* and *Ad Baculum*," *Argumentation* 28 (2014): 301–15.
10. Bart Garssen, "*Ad Hominem* in Disguise: Strategic Manoeuvring with Direct Personal Attacks," *Argumentation and Advocacy* 45 (2009): 207–13; Audrey Yap, "Ad Hominem Fallacies, Bias, and Testimony," *Argumentation* 27 (2013): 97–109.
11. See Johnstone's discussion of Whately in particular. Johnstone, "Locke and Whately," 89–91.
12. Milton Friedman, "On School Vouchers," *St. Croix Review* 32 (1999): 24.
13. Tracy Steffes, *School, Society, and State: A New Education to Govern Modern America, 1880–1940* (Chicago: University of Chicago Press, 2014), 11–12.
14. Paul Manna, *School's In: Federalism and the National Education Agenda* (Washington, DC: Georgetown University Press, 2007), 11–12.
15. David B. Tyack, *The One Best System: A History of American Urban Education* (Cambridge: Harvard University Press, 1974), 284–91.
16. Friedman, "What's Wrong," DVD.
17. Ibid.
18. Originally composed for a concert orchestra, the band would presumably have been playing an arranged version of the piece.
19. Michael B. Katz, *Reconstructing American Education* (Cambridge: Harvard University Press, 1987), 58–59, 109–10.
20. Kenneth Burke, *A Grammar of Motives* (Berkeley: University of California Press, 1969), 59–61, 323–25.
21. Friedman, "What's Wrong," DVD.
22. Ibid.
23. Ibid.
24. Ibid.
25. Ibid.
26. Ibid.
27. Ibid.

28. In this case, my neoliberal diagnosis is meant both as a matter of Friedman's expressed political and philosophical disposition and as a historical observation. Friedman was one of the chief proponents of what has retrospectively been labeled "neoliberalism," and *Free to Choose* was one of his most public contributions to that intellectual movement. David Harvey, *A Brief History of NeoLiberalism* (Oxford: Oxford University Press, 2005), 2.
29. Friedman, "What's Wrong," DVD.
30. Ibid.
31. Each of the discussants is listed with the designation he was given on-screen during the televised debate/discussion except Coons. I have added the fact that he is a law professor. I would also like to thank the University of Chicago's online help chat service, where an anonymous University of Chicago librarian helped me identify the specific room in which this debate/discussion was taped.
32. Friedman, "What's Wrong," DVD.
33. Ibid. Shanker's reputation for rash decision making even appeared in a Woody Allen film. When the protagonist travels into the future, he finds out that the "old world" was destroyed when "a man named Albert Shanker got ahold of a nuclear warhead." Woody Allen, *Sleeper* (Santa Monica: MGM, 2000 [1973]), DVD.
34. Friedman, "What's Wrong," DVD.
35. Ibid.
36. Ibid.
37. Robert Branham, *Debate and Critical Analysis: The Harmony of Conflict* (Hillsdale, NJ: Lawrence Erlbaum Associates, 1991), 116–24.
38. Friedman, "What's Wrong," DVD.
39. Ibid.
40. Friedman, "On School Vouchers," 24.
41. Friedman, "What's Wrong," DVD.
42. George W. Bush, "Remarks on Signing the No Child Left Behind Act of 2001 in Hamilton, Ohio," in *Public Papers of the President of the United States, 2002*, vol. 1 (Washington DC: GPO, 2004), 23–26. This was a talking point Bush had honed on the campaign trail in 2000. George W. Bush, *A Charge to Keep* (New York: William Morrow and Company, 1999), 74.

Chapter 2

1. Terrel H. Bell, *The Thirteenth Man: A Reagan Cabinet Memoir* (New York: The Free Press, 1988), 26.
2. National Commission on Excellence in Education, *A Nation at Risk: The Imperative for Educational Reform* (Washington, DC: Government Printing Office, 1983), 5.
3. All of the quoted material in this paragraph was taken from NCEE, *A Nation at Risk*, 5.
4. Dana Goldstein, *The Teacher Wars: A History of America's Most Embattled Profession* (New York: Doubleday, 2014), 169–74.
5. Holly McIntush, "Defining Education: The Rhetorical Enactment of Ideology in *A Nation at Risk*," *Rhetoric & Public Affairs* 3 (2000): 421. Many others agree with this

assessment; for example: Patricia Albjerg Graham, *Schooling America: How the Public Schools Meet the Nation's Changing Needs* (New York: Oxford University Press, 2005), 153–58.

6. Jal Mehta, "How Paradigms Create Politics: The Transformation of American Education, 1980–2001," *American Education Research Journal* 50 (2013): 314–16.
7. Chester E. Finn, *We Must Take Charge!* (New York: The Free Press, 1991).
8. E. D. Hirsch, *Cultural Literacy: What Every American Needs to Know* (New York: Vintage, 1988), 2–3. Hirsch seems to be drawing upon this specific line: "For our country to function, citizens must be able to reach some common understandings on complex issues, often on short notice and on the basis of conflicting or incomplete evidence." From NCEE, *A Nation at Risk*, 6.
9. McIntush, "Defining Education," 421.
10. Kristen Olsen Lanier, "'Harken to the Sound of the Trumpet': 'A Nation at Risk' as an American Jeremiad" (presentation, Annual Meeting of the American Education Research Association, New Orleans, LA, 2000): 17. Catherine Cornbleth and Esther Gottlieb also recognized the jeremiad in *A Nation at Risk*. Catherine Cornbleth and Esther Gottlieb, "Reform Discourse and Curriculum Reform," *Educational Foundations* 3, no. 3 (Fall 1989): 63–78. For more on the American jeremiad, see Sacvan Bercovitch, *The American Jeremiad* (Madison: University of Wisconsin Press, 1978).
11. For McIntush, Frank Baumgartner's agenda setting accounts for the report's legislative influence, and for Lanier, Sacvan Bercovitch's American jeremiad accounts for *A Nation at Risk*'s social influence. Frank Baumgartner and Bryan Jones, *Agendas and Instability in American Politics* (Chicago: University of Chicago Press, 1993); Sacvan Bercovitch, *The American Jeremiad.*
12. Robert Asen, "Lyndon Baines Johnson and George W. Bush on Education Reform: Ascribing Agency and Responsibility Through Key Policy Terms," *Rhetoric & Public Affairs* 15 (2012): 291–92.
13. William Benoit, *Accounts Excuses, and Apologies: A Theory of Image Restoration* (Albany: State University of New York Press, 1995), 2.
14. Aristotle breaks *ethos* down into three parts, *eunoia* (goodwill), *arête* (virtue or excellence), and *phronesis* (practical wisdom). Aristotle, *On Rhetoric: A Theory of Civic Discourse*, trans. George A. Kennedy (New York: Oxford University Press, 2007). See also Michael J. Hyde, "Rhetorically, We Dwell," in *The Ethos of Rhetoric*, ed. by Michael J. Hyde and Calvin O. Schrag (Columbia: University of South Carolina Press, 2004), xiii–xxvii.
15. Chaim Perelman and L. Olbrechts-Tyteca, *The New Rhetoric: A Treatise on Argumentation* (Notre Dame, IA: University of Notre Dame Press, 1969), 301, 314–15.
16. George A. Kennedy, *The Art of Rhetoric in the Roman World* (Princeton: Princeton University Press, 1972), 114.
17. Graham, *Schooling America*, 167–71.
18. Thomas Toch, *In the Name of Excellence: The Struggle to Reform the Nation's Schools, Why It's Failing, and What Should Be Done* (New York: Oxford, 1991), 14–16.

19. NCEE, *A Nation at Risk*, 9.
20. Ibid., quoted description of the report is from the commission's letter to Secretary Bell, included at the beginning of the report.
21. Scholars often remark on the rhetorical nature of the report, usually crediting the report's success to its rhetoric despite its policy content. For example, see Graham, *Schooling America*, 155, 157–58.
22. NCEE, *A Nation at Risk*, 11.
23. Ibid., 6.
24. Ibid.
25. All of the quoted material in this paragraph was taken from NCEE, *A Nation at Risk*, 5.
26. Ibid.
27. Ibid., 8.
28. Ibid., 5.
29. *A Nation at Risk* rests much of its case for educational failure on declining SAT scores. Many critics have rejected that account, arguing instead that the declines were a result of the democratization of public schooling and university attendance, which had resulted in greater numbers of students taking the SATs. David C. Berliner and Bruce Biddle, *The Manufactured Crisis: Myths, Fraud, and the Attack on the American Public Schools* (New York: Basic Books, 1996), 13–65.
30. NCEE, *A Nation at Risk*, 5.
31. Ibid.
32. Ibid., 8.
33. William V. Spanos, *America's Shadow: An Anatomy of Empire* (Minneapolis: University of Minnesota Press, 2000), 15–17, 128.
34. NCEE, *A Nation at Risk*, 11.
35. Suzy Harris, *The Governance of Education: How Neo-Liberalism is Transforming Policy and Practice* (London: Continuum, 2007), 21–23.
36. Lawrence Cremin, *The Transformation of the School: Progressivism in American Education, 1876–1957* (New York: Knopf, 1961), vi–viii.
37. Graham, *Schooling America*.
38. Perelman and Olbrechts-Tyteca, *The New Rhetoric*, 301, 314–15.
39. William A. Benoit and Kimberly A. Kennedy, "On Reluctant Testimony," *Communication Quarterly* 47, no. 4 (1999): 385–6.
40. McIntush, "Defining Education," 427.
41. Lanier, "Harken," 17–19.
42. Wayne C. Booth, *The Rhetoric of Fiction* (Chicago: University of Chicago Press, 1983), 211–14.
43. NCEE, *A Nation at Risk*, from Letter to Secretary Bell.
44. Ibid., 5–6.
45. Ibid., 5.
46. Ibid., 6.
47. Ibid., 8.

48. All quotations for this paragraph are from NCEE, *A Nation at Risk*, 6.
49. Ibid., 5.
50. Ibid., 8–9. The italics are the NCEE's.
51. Labaree suggests that this particular tension cannot be resolved, but is endemic to how Americans talk about their schools. David F. Labaree, "School Syndrome: Understanding the USA's Magical Belief That Schooling Can Somehow Improve Society, Promote Access, and Preserve Advantage," *Journal of Curriculum Studies* 44, no. 2 (2012): 143–63.
52. NCEE, *A Nation at Risk*, from Letter to Secretary Bell.
53. Goldstein, *The Teacher Wars*, 174.
54. NCEE, *A Nation at Risk*, from Letter to Secretary Bell.
55. Goldstein, *The Teacher Wars*, 166.
56. Rebecca A. Kuehl, "The Rhetorical Presidency and 'Accountability' in Education Reform: Comparing the Presidential Rhetoric of Ronald Reagan and George W. Bush," *Southern Communication Journal* 77, no. 4 (2012): 341–42.
57. NCEE, *A Nation at Risk*, from Letter to Secretary Bell.

Chapter 3

1. Patricia Albjerg Graham, *Schooling America: How the Public Schools Meet the Nation's Changing Needs* (New York: Oxford University Press, 2005), 155–60.
2. Douglas S. Reed, *Building the Federal Schoolhouse: Localism and the American Education State* (New York: Oxford University Press, 2014), 189–92.
3. Jonathan Kozol, *Death at an Early Age: The Destruction of the Hearts and Minds of Negro Children in the Boston Public Schools* (Boston: Houghton Mifflin, 1967).
4. Jonathan Kozol, *Savage Inequalities: Children in America's Schools* (New York: Crown Publishers, 1991), 2.
5. *Publishers Weekly* 238, no. 43 (1991): cover–1; John F. Baker, "An Issue Where Publishers Should Lead The Way," *Publishers Weekly* 238, no. 43 (1991): 2. This advertising revenue figure is in 1991 dollars; it is not adjusted for inflation.
6. Quotes from *Publishers Weekly*, cover.
7. For example, Gene I. Maeroff labels Kozol's comments on desegregation a "subcontext" of the book. Gene I. Maeroff, "Plea for Educational Equality," *Christian Science Monitor*, October 21, 1991, 13.
8. "Publishers Weekly Cover Hails Book," *New York Times*, September 19, 1991, C20.
9. George Bush, "Exchange with Reporters, October 2, 1991," *Public Papers of the President of the United States, 1991*, vol. 2 (Washington, DC: GPO, 1992), 1246–48; George Bush, "Remarks to Students and Faculty at Alice Deal Junior High School, October 1, 1991," *Public Papers of the President of the United States, 1991*, vol. 2 (Washington, DC: GPO, 1992), 1239–42.
10. George Bush, "Remarks to the Department of Education's 1990–1991 Blue Ribbon Schools, September 25, 1991," *Public Papers of the President of the United States, 1991*, vol. 2 (Washington, DC: GPO, 1992), 1213–15.

11. George Bush, "Remarks to the Ohio Education Community, November 25, 1991," *Public Papers of the President of the United States, 1991*, vol. 2 (Washington, DC: GPO, 1992), 1508–11.
12. Quotes from *Publishers Weekly*, cover.
13. Robert Wilson, "'Savage' Indictment of Inequality in America's Schools," *USA Today*, October 18, 1991, 4D.
14. First quotes: Andrew Hacker, "Why the Rich Get Smarter," *New York Times*, October 6, 1991, 7; second quote: Herbert Mitgang, "Books of the Times; Shortchanging the Nation's Schools," *New York Times*, September 25, 1991, C21.
15. Jonathan Kozol, *The Shame of the Nation: The Restoration of Apartheid Schooling in America* (New York: Three Rivers Press, 2005).
16. Kozol, *The Shame*, 238–40. Gary Orfield is more generous to political leaders, attributing resegregation during the 1990s and 2000s to a lack of politic will among constituents: Gary Orfield, "Conclusion: Going Forward," in *Lesson in Integration: Realizing the Promise of Racial Diversity in American Schools*, eds. Erica Frankenberg and Gary Orfield (Cambridge: Harvard Education Press, 2012), 219. Dana Goldstein notes that, after *Brown v. Board*, administrators and school boards across the country sought various alternatives for court-ordered desegregation aside from integration through busing. Dana Goldstein, *The Teacher Wars: A History of America's Most Embattled Profession* (New York: Doubleday, 2014), 175, 179–82.
17. Raquel Farmer-Hinton, Joi D. Lewis, Lori D. Patton, and Ishwanzya D. Rivers, "Dear Mr. Kozol. . . . Four African American Women Scholars and the Re-Authoring of Savage Inequalities," *Teachers College Record* 115 (2013): 1–38.
18. Kenneth Burke, *A Grammar of Motives* (Berkeley: University of California Press, 1969), 503. The italics are Burke's.
19. Leah Ceccarelli, *On the Frontiers of Science: An American Rhetoric of Exploration and Exploitation* (East Lansing: Michigan State University Press, 2013), 19.
20. Emily Dickinson, *The Poems of Emily Dickinson: Reading Edition*, ed. R. W. Franklin (Cambridge: Belknap Press, 2005).
21. Ceccarelli, *On the Frontiers*, 20.
22. George W. Bush, "Remarks on Arrival at the White House and an Exchange with Reporters," *Public Papers of the President of the United States, 2001*, vol. 1 (Washington, DC: GPO, 2003). Gerhard Peters and John T. Woolley, *The American Presidency Project*. http://www.presidency.ucsb.edu/ws/?pid=63346.
23. Peter Ford, "Europe Cringes at Bush 'Crusade' Against Terrorism," *Christian Science Monitor*, September 19, 2001, http://www.csmonitor.com/2001/0919/p12s2-woeu.html.
24. George Lakoff's work is probably best known, but the academic study of metaphors precedes it considerably. George Lakoff and Mark Johnson, *Metaphors We Live By*, 2nd ed. (Chicago: University of Chicago Press, 2005); Michael Osborn, "Archetypal Metaphor in Rhetoric: The Light-Dark Family," *Quarterly Journal of Speech* 53 (1967): 115–26.
25. P. F. Strawson, *Freedom and Resentment and Other Essays* (1974; repr., New York: Routledge, 2008), 1–28.

26. Michael Osborn, "In Defense of Broad Mythic Criticism," *Communication Studies* 41 (1990): 121–22.
27. Kozol, *Savage Inequalities*, 7, 10, 12, 37.
28. Ibid., 8, 10.
29. Debra Hawhee, "Looking into Aristotle's Eyes: Toward a Theory of Rhetorical Vision," *Advances in the History of Rhetoric* 14 (2011): 159.
30. Hawhee, "Aristotle's Eyes," 142.
31. Kozol, *Savage Inequalities*, 7.
32. Ibid., 7
33. Ibid., 10, 12.
34. Ibid., 15.
35. Kozol implies that the Martin Luther King Jr. Bridge separates East St. Louis's black population from white populations in and around St. Louis, but because the bridge connects downtown St. Louis to East St. Louis, this characterization is a stretch. Kozol's sometimes loose interpretations of local geography are part of how he achieves such a compelling narrative in *Savage Inequalities*.
36. Ibid., 10–11.
37. Ibid., 24.
38. Ibid.
39. Ibid., 27–29.
40. Ibid., 30–32.
41. Ibid., 30.
42. Ibid., 31.
43. Offering their own counternarratives of life in East St. Louis in response to Kozol's "caricaturization," Raquel Farmer-Hinton et al. resist and "complicate" Kozol's description of East St. Louis in *Savage Inequalities*. Concerned that "future educators who read *Savage Inequalities*" might "misunderstand urban students and families as subjects who need to be saved or strategically avoid urban teaching placements," Farmer-Hinton and her colleagues point to the "deficit discourse" in *Savage Inequalities* as the textual origin of the disenfranchisement I point to here. Farmer-Hinton et al., "Dear Mr. Kozol. . . . ," 1–38.
44. This is not blank reportage, but actually a bit of embellishment for the sake of his argument. The bluffs themselves are actually set back from East St. Louis. The town is not surrounded by the cliffs his descriptions bring to mind. Kozol, *Savage Inequalities*, 11.
45. Ibid., 7.
46. Ibid., 12.
47. Ibid., 224.
48. Ibid., 224–25.
49. Ibid., 10–11, 37.
50. Ibid., 224.
51. Ibid., 87.
52. Ibid., 85–86.

53. Ibid., 92–94.
54. Ibid., 93.
55. Aside from the dramatic socioeconomic differences, Kozol notes that "the last white families left" North Lawndale sometime "between 1960 and 1970" and that New Trier High School is "1.3 percent black." Kozol, *Savage Inequalities*, 42, 66.
56. Ibid., 41–42, 65.
57. Ibid., 42–43, 65.
58. Ibid., 233.
59. Ibid.
60. *Oxford English Dictionary Online*, s.v. "soil, v. 1," accessed May 20, 2013, http://www.oed.com/view/Entry/183973.
61. Kozol, *Savage Inequalities*, 38–39.
62. *Death at an Early Age* and the book Kozol published immediately before *Savage Inequalities, Rachel and Her Children*, especially convey his position that racial isolation bears a causal relationship with social problems in the United States. Jonathan Kozol, *Rachel and Her Children: Homeless Families in America* (New York: Fawcett Columbine, 1989).
63. Kozol, *Savage Inequalities*, 17, 30.
64. *Milliken, Governor of Michigan, et al. v. Bradley et al.*, 418 U.S. 717 (1974).
65. Kozol, *Savage Inequalities*, 13.
66. Wendy Kopp, "An Argument and Plan for the Creation of a Teacher Corps" (bachelor's thesis, Princeton University, 1989), 1.
67. Kopp, "An Argument and Plan," 47.

Chapter 4

1. George W. Bush, "Remarks on Signing the No Child Left Behind Act of 2001 in Hamilton, Ohio, January 8, 2002," *Public Papers of the President of the United States, 2002*, vol. 1 (Washington, DC: GPO, 2004), 23–26.
2. The ESEA typified the "access" era of education policy, serving to increase access to educational opportunities for as many students as possible. Patricia Albjerg Graham, *Schooling America: How the Public Schools Meet the Nation's Changing Needs* (New York: Oxford University Press, 2005), 132–37.
3. Meira Levinson, *No Citizen Left Behind* (Cambridge: Harvard University Press, 2012); Jal Mehta, *The Allure of Order: High Hopes, Dashed Expectations, and The Troubled Quest to Remake American Schooling* (New York: Oxford University Press, 2013); Diane Ravitch, *Reign of Error: The Hoax of the Privatization Movement and the Danger to America's Public Schools* (New York: Knopf, 2013); Douglas S. Reed, *Building the Federal Schoolhouse: Localism and the American Education State* (New York: Oxford University Press, 2014).
4. Lee W. Anderson, *Congress in the Classroom: From the Cold War to "No Child Left Behind"* (University Park: The Pennsylvania State University Press, 2007); Graham, *Schooling America*; Patrick J. McGuinn, *No Child Left Behind and the Transformation*

of Federal Education Policy, 1965–2005 (Lawrence: University of Kansas Press, 2006); Jesse H. Rhodes, *An Education in Politics: The Origins and Evolution of No Child Left Behind* (Ithaca: Cornell University Press, 2012).

5. Frank Lentricchia, *Criticism and Social Change* (Chicago: University of Chicago Press, 1985); Jack Selzer, *Kenneth Burke in Greenwich Village: Conversing with the Moderns 1915–1931* (Madison: University of Wisconsin Press, 1996).
6. Kenneth Burke, *A Grammar of Motives* (Berkeley: University of California Press, 1969), 406–8; Kenneth Burke, *Permanence and Change* (Berkeley: University of California Press, 1954), 14–17; Kenneth Burke, "The Rhetoric of Hitler's Battle," in *The Philosophy of Literary Form* (Berkeley: University of California Press, 1973), 191–221. "The Rhetoric of Hitler's Battle" was first published in the *Southern Review* in 1939, but is most commonly read as reprinted in *The Philosophy of Literary Form.*
7. Burke, *A Grammar of Motives*, 406–8.
8. Kenneth Burke, *Language as Symbolic Action: Essays on Life, Literature, and Method* (Berkeley: University of California Press, 1966), 3–9.
9. To follow the development of the ESEA's statement of policy, see Elementary and Secondary Education Act of 1965, Pub. L. No. 89-10, 64 Stat. 1100 (1965), § 201; Augustus F. Hawkins–Robert T. Stafford Elementary and Secondary School Improvement Amendments of 1988, Pub. L. No. 100-297, 102 Stat. 130 (1988), § 1001; Improving America's Schools Act of 1994, Pub. L. No. 103-382, 108 Stat. 3518 (1994), § 1001; No Child Left Behind Act of 2001, Pub. L. No. 107-110, 115 Stat. 1425 (2002), § 1001.
10. Improving America's Schools Act of 1994, § 1001.b.4-5. A quick read over President Bill Clinton's signing statement for the IASA reveals the rhetoric of accountability on strong display as Clinton described the new law. William J. Clinton, "Remarks on Signing the Improving America's Schools Act of 1994 in Framingham, Massachusetts, October 20, 1994," *Public Papers of the President of the United States, 1994*, vol. 2 (Washington, DC: GPO, 1995), 1811–15.
11. Anderson, *Congress in the Classroom*, 130–31; Rhodes, *An Education in Politics*, 132–33.
12. Rhodes, *An Education in Politics*, 140.
13. Burke, *A Grammar of Motives*, 406.
14. Bush, "Remarks on Signing the No Child Left Behind Act of 2001," 23–26.
15. For some discussion see Robert Asen, "Lyndon Baines Johnson and George W. Bush on Education Reform: Ascribing Agency and Responsibility Through Key Policy Terms," *Rhetoric & Public Affairs* 15 (2012): 298–317.
16. Bush, "Remarks on Signing the No Child Left Behind Act of 2001," 23–26.
17. Burke, *A Grammar of Motives*, 406.
18. No Child Left Behind Act of 2001, Pub. L. No. 107-110, 115 Stat. 1425 (2002), § 1001.1-12.
19. Ibid., § 1001.
20. Ibid., § 1001.1.
21. Ibid., § 1001.4.
22. Ibid., § 1001.7.

23. Paul Manna, *School's In: Federalism and the National Education Agenda* (Washington, DC: Georgetown University Press, 2007).
24. This is a habit that recurred at the signing of the original Elementary and Secondary Education Act of 1965, the founding of the Department of Education, and the signing of NCLB. Bush, "Remarks on Signing the No Child Left Behind Act of 2001," 23–26; Jimmy Carter, "Department of Education Organization Act: Statement on Signing S. 210 Into Law, October 17, 1979," *Public Papers of the President of the United States, 1979*, vol. 2 (Washington, DC: GPO, 1980), 1959; Lyndon B. Johnson, "Remarks in Johnson City, Tex., Upon Signing the Elementary and Secondary Education Bill, April 11, 1965," *Public Papers of the President of the United States, 1965*, vol. 1 (Washington, DC: GPO, 1966), 413.
25. P. F. Strawson, *Freedom and Resentment and Other Essays* (1974; repr., New York: Routledge, 2008), 1–28.
26. Burke, *A Grammar of Motives*, 406.
27. Ibid.
28. No Child Left Behind Act of 2001, § 1111.g.2.
29. Ibid., § 1111.b.2.C.ii, iv.
30. Ibid., § 1111.b.2.C.i.
31. Ibid., § 1111.b.2.G.iii.
32. Ibid., § 1111.b.2.C.ii, v.
33. For example, see No Child Left Behind Act of 2001 § 1111.b.3.C, a list of requirements for academic assessments given by the states. Although NCLB seems to hold open the possibility for assessments other than standardized tests, subpoint iv assumes that the technical viability of the assessments used to determine AYP can be established by the assurance of "test publishers." Indeed, NCLB resulted in testing so effectively that scholars often describe it as requiring standardized tests by not providing any other viable option. See, for example, Graham, *Schooling America*, 188–89.
34. No Child Left Behind Act of 2001, § 1111.b.2.D.
35. Ibid., § 1111.b.2.C.v.II.
36. Burke, *A Grammar of Motives*, 406.
37. *Oxford English Dictionary Online*, s.v. "corrective," http://www.oed.com.
38. No Child Left Behind Act of 2001, § 1116.c.2.
39. Ibid., § 1117.b.1.
40. Burke, *A Grammar of Motives*, 406.
41. Ibid.
42. No Child Left Behind Act of 2001, § 1111.h.1.C.i-viii.
43. "ESSA Loosens Reins on Teacher Evaluations, Qualifications," *Education Week* 35 (2016): 14; "ESSA Law Broadens Definition of School Success," *Education Week* 35 (2016): 15.

Chapter 5

1. In 2008, the Department of Education under the Bush Administration began accepting waivers from states struggling to meet NCLB's requirements. See Sam Dillon, "US

Eases 'No Child' Law as Applied to Some States," *New York Times*, March 19, 2008, 11. In 2011, the Department of Education under the Obama Administration universalized this policy, essentially ending NCLB as a school-closing law. See Sam Dillon, "Obama to Waive Parts of No Child Left Behind," *New York Times*, September 22, 2011, http://www.nytimes.com/2011/09/23/education/23educ.html?_r=0. The term "do-nothing Congress" comes from Harry Truman's presidential campaign against Thomas Dewey and Strom Thurmond in 1948. It described the 80th Congress of the United States, a governing body that passed some thirty times the number of laws as the 113th. Steven R. Goldzwig, *Truman's Whistle-Stop Campaign* (College Station: Texas A&M University Press, 2008), 9–10, 107–8.

2. David S. Broder, "The Long Road to Reform: Negotiations Forge Education Legislation," *Washington Post*, December 17, 2001; Patrick J. McGuinn, *No Child Left Behind and the Transformation of Federal Education Policy 1965–2005* (Lawrence: The University of Kansas Press, 2006), 166.
3. Diane Jean Schemo, "Kennedy Demands Full Funding for School Bill," *New York Times*, April 7, 2004. Kennedy had been referred to as one of NCLB's "Big Four" legislative backers. See, for example, Siobhan Gorman, "Bipartisan Schoolmates," *Education Next* 2 (Summer 2002): 39.
4. For example, in March of 2010 the *New York Times* published a series of letters to the editor welcoming Ravitch's change of heart. "An Educator's Change of Heart," *New York Times*, March 8, 2010.
5. Diane Ravitch, "Why I Changed My Mind About School Reform," *Wall Street Journal*, March 9, 2010, http://www.wsj.com/articles/SB100014240527487048693045751094433305343962. The *Wall Street Journal* op-ed was timed to release along with her book on the subject: Diane Ravitch, *The Death and Life of the Great American School System: How Testing and Choice are Undermining Education* (New York: Basic Books, 2010). In 2007, Ravitch had announced her doubts about NCLB in a *New York Times* op-ed, but at that time she still maintained that the law could be salvaged. See Diane Ravitch, "Get Congress Out of the Classroom," *New York Times*, October 3, 2007.
6. Creating conservative scholarship is not the same as being a Republican. Ravitch outs herself as a lifelong Democrat in the introduction to *The Death and Life of the Great American School System*. Nonetheless, her scholarship during the 1970s, '80s, and '90s was decidedly conservative. Ravitch, *The Death and Life*, 7.
7. Diane Ravitch, *The Revisionists Revised: A Critique of the Radical Attack on the Schools* (New York: Basic Books, 1978); Diane Ravitch, *The Troubled Crusade: American Education, 1945–1980* (New York: Basic Books, 1983); *Diane Ravitch, Left Back: A Century of Failed School Reforms* (New York: Simon & Schuster, 2000).
8. Referencing James C. Scott's work, she describes the process of learning to "see like a state" at the Department of Education. Ravitch, *The Death and Life*, 10.
9. Ravitch, "Why I Changed."
10. Carla B. Anderson, "Book Review: The Death and Life of the Great American School System: How Testing and Choice are Undermining Education by Diane Ravitch," *Educational Studies* 47 (2011): 495–98; David Glenn, "Diane Ravitch Would Like to Put

the 'Public' Back in Public Schools," *Chronicle of Higher Education*, March 14, 2010, http://chronicle.com/article/Diane-Ravitch-Wants-the/64586; Arnold L. Mitchell, "Book Review: The Death and Life of the Great American School System: How Testing and Choice are Undermining Education by Diane Ravitch," *History of Education Quarterly* 51 (2011): 424–26; Kathy J. Rho, "Book Review: The Death and Life of the Great American School System: How Testing and Choice are Undermining Education by Diane Ravitch," *Education Review* 14 (2011): 283–89; Debra Viadero, "In New Book, Ravitch Recants Long-Held Beliefs," *Education Week* 29 (2010): 1, 14–15.

11. Joel Klein, *Lessons of Hope: How to Fix Our Schools* (New York: Harper, 2014), 65–76.
12. Up-to-date information about all of these activities can be found on Dr. Ravitch's blog: http://dianeravitch.net and http://dianeravitch.com.
13. Ravitch, *The Death and Life*, 3.
14. For those interested in psychologizing Ravitch's conversion, I recommend Eric Hoffer, *The True Believer: Thoughts on the Nature of Mass Movements* (New York: Harper, 1951).
15. For example, Diane Ravitch, "Clinton's School Plan Is a Good Start, Let's Go Farther," *Wall Street Journal*, January 20, 1999, 22; Diane Ravitch, "Higher, But Hollow, Academic Standards," *New York Times*, February 6, 1999, 15.
16. John Lynch, "'Prepare to Believe': The Creation Museum as Embodied Conversion Narrative," *Rhetoric & Public Affairs* 16 (2014): 3. Rodger M. Payne, *The Self and the Sacred: Conversion and Autobiography in Early American Protestantism* (Knoxville: University of Tennessee Press, 1998), 4–6.
17. I employ *ethos* as the habitation of character. James N. Comas, *Between Politics and Ethics: Toward a Vocative History of English Studies* (Columbia: University of South Carolina Press, 2006), 95–100.
18. Raymond Van Dam, *Remembering Constantine and Milvian Bridge* (New York: Cambridge University Press, 2011), 15–18.
19. For the most agreeable prose, I quote Brian Donovan's translation. Gorgias, "Encomium of Helen," trans. Brian Donovan, *Peitho's Web*, 1999, http://www.classicpersuasion.org/pw/gorgias/helendonovan.htm. To ensure the reliability of Donovan's interpretation, I consulted an earlier translation by Sprague and Diels: Gorgias, "Encomium of Helen," in Rosamund Kent Sprague and Hermann Diels, *The Older Sophists* (Columbia: University of South Carolina Press, 1972), 50–54.
20. Gorgias, "Encomium," trans. by Donovan.
21. Ibid.
22. Ravitch, "Why I Changed."
23. Ibid.
24. Ravitch, *The Death and Life*, 1.
25. Ibid., 110.
26. Ibid., 2.
27. Ibid., 4.
28. Ibid., 3.
29. Gorgias, "Encomium," trans. by Donovan.

30. Ravitch, *The Death and Life*, 3.
31. Ibid., 2.
32. Ibid., 13.
33. Ibid., 2.
34. Ibid., 2.
35. Ravitch is very clear that changing facts justify changing one's mind, and she applies that scenario to her experience: Ravitch, *The Death and Life*, 2.
36. Ibid., 16.
37. The topic comes up only in passing—for example, in her discussion of the failure of the school choice component of NCLB: Ravitch, *The Death and Life*, 99–101.
38. Ravitch, *The Death and Life*, 35.
39. Ibid., 63–64.
40. Ibid., 76.
41. Ibid., 89–90.
42. Ibid., 108.
43. See chapter 4 for a discussion of how failure to meet AYP often resulted in the narrowing of curricula.
44. Ravitch, *The Death and Life*, 152.
45. Ibid., 166.
46. Ibid., 159.
47. Ibid., 160.
48. Ibid., 85.
49. Ibid., 107–8.
50. Ravitch, "Why I Changed."
51. Ravitch, *The Death and Life*, 102.
52. For example, this discomfort was cited as a reason when the Bush administration began issuing exemptions from the consequences of NCLB in 2008. Dillon, "US Eases 'No Child' Law," 11.
53. Ravitch, *The Death and Life*, 13.
54. Barack Obama, "Remarks by the President at Every Student Succeeds Signing Ceremony," *The White House: Office of the Press Secretary*, December 10, 2015, https://www.whitehouse.gov/the-press-office/2015/12/10/remarks-president-every-student-succeeds-act-signing-ceremony.
55. Ravitch is not alone in making this argument, but she does have a bigger public audience than most. See, for example, David F. Labaree, *Someone Has to Fail: The Zero-Sum Game of Public Schooling* (Cambridge: Harvard University Press, 2010).

Chapter 6

1. This is as evidenced by the case studies, picked for the preeminence of their influence. Instances of public blame in the discussion of education exist across the history of public education in the United States, especially as concerns about the health of public education wax and wane. A few obvious examples of this phenomenon include DeWitt Clinton, *An Address to the Benefactors and Friends of the Free School Society of New*

York, Delivered on the Opening of That Institution, in Their New and Spacious Building, on the Eleventh of the Twelfth Month December 1809 (New York: Collins and Perkins, 1810); Arthur Bestor, *Educational Wastelands: The Retreat from Learning in Our Public Schools* (Urbana: University of Illinois Press, 1953); Sloan Wilson, "It's Time to Close Our Carnival," *Life*, March 24, 1958, 36–37.

2. Jurgen Habermas describes a somewhat related phenomenon as it affects governments: Jurgen Habermas, *Legitimation Crisis*, trans. Thomas McCarthy (Boston, MA: Beacon Press, 1973), 23. Mark C. Suchman dissects governmental legitimacy into several parts, the most relevant of which is what he calls "moral legitimacy": Mark C. Suchman, "Managing Legitimacy: Strategic and Institutional Approaches," *Academy of Management Review* 20 (1995): 571–610.
3. Dana Goldstein, *The Teacher Wars: A History of America's Most Embattled Profession* (New York: Doubleday, 2014), 274; Christopher A. Lubienski and Sarah Theule Lubienski, *The Public School Advantage: Why Public Schools Outperform Private Schools* (Chicago: University of Chicago Press, 2014), xi–xv, 133–46; Diane Ravitch, *Reign of Error: The Hoax of the Privatization Movement and the Danger to America's Public Schools* (New York: Knopf, 2013), 310–12. Jesse Rhodes finds the federal government playing a more central role in education policy in the run-up to the passage of NCLB, but through the efforts of "policy entrepreneurs" who become the privatizers other scholars bemoan: Jesse H. Rhodes, *An Education in Politics: The Origins and Evolution of No Child Left Behind* (Ithaca: Cornell University Press, 2014), 183–90.
4. David F. Labaree, *Someone Has to Fail: The Zero-Sum Game of Public Schooling* (Cambridge: Harvard University Press, 2010), 222–27, 243–45; Jal Mehta, *The Allure of Order: High Hopes, Dashed Expectations, and the Troubled Quest to Remake American Schooling* (New York: Oxford University Press, 2013), 5, 34–36.
5. David Arsen, "An Open Letter to Michigan Governor Rick Snyder," April 23, 2013, http://edwp.educ.msu.edu/new-educator/2013/faculty-viewpoint/; *Ravitch, Reign of Error*, 3–10; Dale Russakoff, *The Prize: Who's in Charge of America's Schools* (Boston: Houghton Mifflin Harcourt, 2015).
6. Ravitch, *Reign of Error*, 161–74. For closer analyses of charters in specific city contexts, see as examples: Kristen Buras, *Charter Schools, Race, and Urban Space: Where the Market Meets Grassroots Resistance* (New York: Routledge, 2015); Russakoff, *The Prize*, 1–21, 197–208. The Lubienskis discuss the process by which advocates of school choice have funded university research in support of their political positions: Lubienski and Lubienski, *The Public Schools Advantage*, 136.
7. Mehta, *Allure of Order*, 12.
8. Patricia Albjerg Graham, *Schooling America: How the Public Schools Meet the Nation's Changing Needs* (New York: Oxford University Press, 2005), 2, 153–58.
9. Labaree points to this diversification of the justification for accountability-based policies in the NCLB's statement of purpose: Labaree, *Someone Has to Fail*, 37.
10. The phrase has been credited to Bush's former speechwriter, Michael Gerson: "Leading Bush Speechwriter Resigns," *Fox News*, June 15, 2006, http://www.foxnews.com/story/2006/06/15/leading-bush-speechwriter-resigns.html. However, it is probably

familiar to most from Bush's campaign biography: George W. Bush, *A Charge to Keep* (New York: Morrow, 1999), 233.

11. The phrase is all over the book, but for an example see Bush, *A Charge to Keep*, 24.
12. In her most recent book, Ravitch puts a finer point on the distinction between blaming the public schools and the laws that govern them. Ravitch, *Reign of Error*, 4.
13. Dana Golstein discusses how the generalized sense of education as failing serves as a justification for "tough reforms" like those based in accountability. See Goldstein, *The Teacher Wars*, 168.
14. To be clear, the expert discussion of the Common Core standards did reflect these concerns, but the public, political discussion did not.
15. "Resistance to the Common Core Mounts; Critics Span the Political Spectrum, from Tea Partyers to Union Leaders," *Education Week*, April 23, 2014.
16. Lyndsey Layton, "Common Core Standards Have Critics on Right, Left," *Washington Post*, April 30, 2014.
17. Emma Brown, "Gov. Jindal Attacks Common Core," *Washington Post*, February 6, 2015; Wayne Washington, "Common Core Can be Money Maker," *Atlanta Journal-Constitution*, August 25, 2013.
18. Andrew Ujifusa, "Resistance to Common Core Mounts," *Education Week*, April 28, 2014.
19. "Myths vs. Facts," *Common Core State Standards Initiative*, http://www.corestandards.org/about-the-standards/myths-vs-facts/.
20. "Standards Persist Amid Controversy," *Education Week*, August 6, 2014.
21. Richard Hofstadter, *The Paranoid Style in American Politics: And Other Essays* (New York: Random House, 1967).
22. Karen Tumulty and Lyndsey Layton, "The Culture Wars Come to a Colo. History Course," *Washington Post*, October 6, 2014.
23. Nicholas Garcia, "Why the Tug-of-War for Jefferson County's School Board Isn't Just About Local Classrooms," *Chalkbeat.org*, July 22, 2015, http://co.chalkbeat.org/2015/07/22/why-the-tug-of-war-for-jefferson-countys-school-board-isnt-just-about-local-classrooms/#.VplhXTYqQ5M.
24. Rick M. Green, "Oklahoma Lawmaker Reworking Advanced Placement Bill Says He Supports Program," *Daily Oklahoman*, February 18, 2015.
25. Lubienski and Lubienski, *The Public School Advantage*, 136–37.
26. Eric A. Hanushek, Paul E. Peterson, and Ludger Woessmann, *Not Just a Problem for Other People's Children* (Cambridge, MA: Program on Education Policy and Governance, 2014), 30.
27. Ibid., 31.
28. The Department of Education Reform at the University of Arkansas is a nearly identical entity, so much so that this criticism does not bear repeating.

Chapter 7

1. Shirley Hufstedler, "Remarks by Shirley M. Hufstedler, Secretary of Education to the Illinois Education Association, Friday, February 29, 1980, Chicago, Illinois," Record

Group 441, A1 E1 130.74.13.01, Box 20, National Archives at College Park, College Park, MD. Quote from pages 14–15.

2. Kenneth Burke, *The Philosophy of Literary Form* (Berkeley: University of California Press, 1973), 293–304.
3. Aristotle, *On Rhetoric: A Theory of Civic Discourse*, trans. George A. Kennedy (New York: Oxford University Press, 2007), 81.
4. Ibid., 80–81.
5. US Department of Education, "Programs: National Blue Ribbon Schools Program," http://www2.ed.gov/programs/nclbbrs/index.html.
6. George W. Bush, "Remarks at Boston Latin School in Boston, Massachusetts, January 8, 2002," *Public Papers of the President of the United States, 2002*, vol. 1 (Washington, DC: GPO, 2004), 30–33.
7. Aristotle recounts this famous adage from Socrates in his discussion of praise and blame. See Aristotle, *On Rhetoric*, 79–80.
8. J. Michael Sproule, *Propaganda and Democracy: The American Experience of Media and Mass Persuasion* (Cambridge: Cambridge University Press, 1997), 135.
9. US Department of Education, "Programs: Race to the Top Fund," http://www2.ed.gov/programs/racetothetop/index.html.
10. "The Fight Over Education in Washington," *New York Times*, July 31, 2010; "Losing States in Race to Top Scramble to Meet Promises; Ambitious Promises During Contest Leave Some Who Lost Out Scrambling," *Education Week* 30 (2011): 24; Alyson Klain, "'Race to Top' Standards Link Questioned; Some in Congress Worry Federal Intrusion Ahead Through Money for Testing," *Education Week* 29 (2010): 13; Michele McNeil, "Criteria Seen as Too Restrictive in Quest for 'Race to Top' Funds," *Education Week* 29 (2010): 23; Stephen Sawchuk, "Two State Unions Balking at 'Race to Top' Plans," *Education Week* 29 (2010): 1.
11. For a discussion of what I mean by an interpretive tradition, see Gerald L. Bruns, *Inventions: Writing, Textuality, and Understanding in Literary History* (New Haven: Yale University Press, 1982).
12. Michael J. Steudeman, "Indeterminacy, Incipiency, and Attitudes: Materialist Oscillation in the 2012 Chicago Teachers' Strike," *Quarterly Journal of Speech* 101 (2015): 509–33.
13. Rosa A. Eberly, *Citizen Critics: Literary Public Spheres* (Urbana: University of Illinois Press, 2000).
14. Dana Goldstein, *The Teacher Wars: A History of America's Most Embattled Profession* (New York: Doubleday, 2014), 274; David F. Labaree, *Someone Has to Fail: The Zero-Sum Game of Public Schooling* (Cambridge: Harvard University Press, 2010).

Acknowledgments

Some words of praise to inspirit the reader of a book about blame—

This is a first book. It was raised as much as written. The ideas at its center were developed at The Pennsylvania State University, where they benefited from the generosity of the Department of Communication Arts & Sciences, the Department of English, the College of Education, the College of the Liberal Arts, the Institute for the Arts and Humanities, the Center for Democratic Deliberation, Webster's Bookstore Café, and all of the scholars who also called those places home.

More than anyone, I would like to thank my advisor, Thomas W. Benson, for his thoughts and patience, and for modeling the very best of both academia and humanity. Those familiar with the intellectual acuity of Rosa A. Eberly, Jeremy Engels, Keith Gilyard, and Kirt H. Wilson will recognize their influence throughout this book and feel as grateful for it as I do. William A. Boyd, David A. Gamson, Dana L. Mitra, and Stephanie Serriere all guided different aspects of my exploration of the wide world of education scholarship, and I hope this book reflects the excellence of their instruction.

At several points during the writing process I reached out to scholars I admire who read drafts and offered timely advice. Thank you to Robert Asen, Leah Ceccarelli, Cheryl Glenn, Debra Hawhee, J. Michael Hogan,

Kyle Jensen, Michele Kennerly, Meira Levinson, Gordon R. Mitchell, Jack Selzer, and Dave Tell for advising, challenging, and sometimes—I can think of no better way to put this—"unstucking" me.

The academic life has bestowed upon me a multitude of smart and patient friends. Here are the ones who put up with the most from me while I worked on this project: Brian Amsden, John Belk, Bryan Blankfield, Kristina Brezicha, Holly Gates, Cory Geraths, Hillary A. Jones, Roi Kawai, Alexandria Lockett, Ersula Ore, Joseph Rhodes, Sarah RudeWalker, William O. Saas, Jessica Sheffield, Frank Stec, Michael J. Steudeman, and Sarah Summers. Thanks to all.

Although this book was started at Penn State, it was finished at the University of North Texas, where I am grateful to my colleagues and students in the Department of Communication Studies who have made Denton a fantastic place to live and work.

For me, college policy debate was a life-changing experience. The intellectual who wrote this book did not exist before his future debate partner dragged him to a beginning-of-the-year meeting. Thank you, Christopher Wood. Also, thank you, M. Ilon Lauer, for teaching me how to think critically and thank you, Josh Averbeck and Amber Davisson, for assisting him in that challenging endeavor.

Finally, I would like to express my appreciation for my family, who have supported me throughout this nigh maniacal undertaking. My parents, Lisa, Rick, Julie, and Tom, always encourage me to pursue my passions. My son, Brendon, always asks me the best questions. My wife, Rachel, always gives me the best answers. I owe you more than I could express short of writing a book of praise.

About the Author

Mark Hlavacik is Assistant Professor of Communication Studies at the University of North Texas in Denton. He specializes in rhetoric and public deliberation and his research focuses on contemporary and historical controversies over education policy in the United States.

In addition to *Assigning Blame*, Dr. Hlavacik has published work about the emergence of teachers union rhetoric, the opt-out movement, presidential rhetoric, and civic engagement on college campuses and in college debate. His work has appeared in *Rhetoric & Public Affairs*, *Communication Education*, *Education Policy Analysis Archives*, and *Cultural Studies <=> Critical Methodologies*. Alongside his work on the rhetoric of blame, Dr. Hlavacik is pursuing research concerning the rhetoric of education policy in the executive branch and the relationship between public education and propaganda analysis.

Dr. Hlavacik earned his master's and doctoral degrees in the Department of Communication Arts & Sciences at The Pennsylvania State University. He earned his bachelor's degree in history with an endorsement in secondary education from Western Illinois University, where he was trained in a traditional teacher education program. He completed his student teaching in the Chicago Public Schools at Benito Juarez High School while coaching high school debate at Gwendolyn Brooks College Preparatory Academy.

Index